SeniorSex

Answers to Your Questions From a Geriatric Gynecologist

CHICAGO PUBLIC LIBRARY
HAROLD WASHINGTON LIBRARY
BUSINESS /SCIENCE/TECHNOLOGY
400 S. STATE ST. 4TH FLOOR
CHICAGO IL 60605

SeniorSex

answers to your questions from a
geriatric gynecologist

Daniel Laury, M.D.

Hatala Geroproducts • Greentop, Missouri

Copyright ©2009 Daniel Laury
All rights reserved under
International and Pan-American copyright conventions
Published in the United States of America
by Hatala Geroproducts, Greentop, MO 63546

(pop 427)

09 08 07 06 05 1 2 3 4 5

SeniorSex: Answers to Your Questions From a Geriatric Gynecologist
by Daniel Laury

ISBN-13: 978-1-933167-45-9
LCCN: 2008939620

Author's Disclaimer: The information in this book is felt to be accurate at the time of writing. Though great care was used in bringing this project together, the art and science of medicine is constantly changing. Necessarily, the information contained herein may become obsolete. The techniques that I write about may not apply to all readers, some may be dangerous or inappropriate depending on ethical, medical or anatomical constraints. Use your best judgement, consult with your health provider and do you own homework. I use real people and situations to improve readability however I have also taken the liberty of changing things to protect the identity of my patients. My book website http://www.seniorsexmd.com allows you access to more information including a blog, Q & A, email access to me, other contact information, etc.
  Since I have not personally had the opportunity to establish a doctor:patient relationship with you, I can not advise you to follow any of this book's recommendations. Before trying anything in this book you are advised to seek permission from your own health care provider.

Cover Design: Age Positive Design
Cover and Interior Photos: Steve Luker
Composition: Age Positive Editorial Services

Acknowledgement

Spending well over a year on this book I need to apologize to and recognize the many people who were involved in this project. My staff were particularly patient with me especially when I asked for their help. At home, Lisa tolerated many lonely evenings as I wrote up the various drafts of this manuscript. She was always supportive and I will always appreciate her positive energy. Many friends contributed to the finished book in their individual fashion. I embarrassed many of them, asking them questions of a personal nature usually only broached after an evening of drinking. Following in the footsteps of my father, this book continues his tradition of sexual education. My sister, Valerie, was ever enthusiastic and believed in me. Finally, I owe an enormous debt to my patients who contributed to all of these questions. Without them, none of this would have come to fruition. Through their travails and honesty I was able to learn about a world which has been largely ignored. This book is dedicated to the seniors of the world by contributing to an improvement in their sexual lives. Thank you all for your unwavering support.

Daniel Laury, MD
February 2009

Table of Contents

Foreword

1	About the book	13
2	What is normal?	23
3	When sex doesn't work	41
4	Sexual pain disorders	63
5	Partner issues	73
6	Social and privacy challenges	89
7	Psychological issues	95
8	Medications	109
9	Hormonal, systemic and medical problems	129
10	What to do?	143
11	Other vaginal issues	151
12	The dangers of sex	157
13	Resources	163

Glossary	175
Index	184

1
About the Book

1.1 How did I come up with the title?

I wanted something snappy and memorable as well as descriptive. I considered various alternatives, including "Seniors, Sex and How To". "Sex After ___" (fill in an age) would limit the folks who would benefit from reading this book. And "ElderSex" and "OlderSex" sounded faintly negative. So, I settled on SeniorSex, which I think covers most of the bases.

1.2 Dr. Laury, why did you write this book?

I feel that there is a strong need for a book like this. Seniors in general have been ignored in terms of their sexuality. When questions arise, where are older folks expected to get quality information? On the other hand, there is plenty of misinformation available, including the internet, friends, outdated books, etc. In addition, many patients tell me that other doctors "don't listen" to them or just don't even bring up sexual issues. It is hard for some people to start talking about sexual subjects – this applies to patients as well as doctors. I deal with these issues daily. When the subject comes up in the office settings, I am often told that I am the only one who ever discussed this. That is truly a shame. Approximately 10 to 20% of sexually dysfunctional women actually looked to their health care providers for help.[1] Usually the sooner I hear about a problem the better the response I can expect from treatment.

1.3 Why should I read this book?

I would hope that there is information here that you can use. I have put together answers to common questions that are based on my experience as well as scientific research. If I help even one person, it would have made writing this book worthwhile. These questions come up daily and as I found myself repeating myself in the office, I decided to put them down on paper.

1.4 How do I get my doctor to talk to me about my sexuality?

The simple answer is just to ask him or her. In reality, that may be difficult for many reasons. I recommend that my patients set up an appointment specifically to talk about "sexual problems". This helps me schedule enough time for them. It also gives the staff just enough information to schedule an appointment without having to embarrass anyone by revealing all the gory details. All too often, people schedule for other reasons such as vaginitis, fatigue or pelvic pain when the real issue is sexual. If we need to talk sex, then it is important to alert me to that fact.

There are also different types of providers. In some group settings, you may end up seeing many different practitioners. This may be to your advantage if you know that you are unlikely to see that same person again or they are so busy that they will forget you by the next visit. Other patients prefer their "own" doctor. My office is run this way. I try to remember my patients, their family, history, interests, etc. Obviously, the people who come to me prefer that setting and may be more comfortable discussing difficult issues with me. Another advantage is that I can provide follow up care if we need to try different therapies. Interestingly, even though I ask if there are sexual problems at least annually, it sometimes takes a few years before someone is able to share their issues with me.

Some patients prefer the older providers because they are closer in age to them or perhaps they represent experience. Some prefer younger docs because they feel that they have the latest information. The truth is that if the practitioner is knowledgeable and accessible (meaning that they are emotionally approachable) they are likely to be of great help. I have been accused of looking too young for the last fifteen years. The joke here in Medford, Oregon was that they picked the youngest doctor to give the senior sex lecture.

1.5 Why is hard to get info or to talk about sex?

Often talking about sexuality is difficult from a patient's perspective. It involves putting a lot of trust in the provider and the office setting. There are issues surrounding sexuality that range from embarrassment to inability to even formulate a question. For example, how does one ask a doctor if masturbation is normal? Or, how do you find out how many times a month folks have sex normally? And, is it appropriate to call your breasts boobs? Often a provider is very busy and time limited. As a patient, you tend to be quite tuned in to picking this up so you may not want to "bother" the doctor with your concerns. Sometimes, after gathering your courage, you actually ask a sensitive question. Then the provider doesn't feel comfortable discussing it or they might not even have the right answers for you. We also have to deal with assumptions and expectations. Many providers assume that an older person is not having sex. Many of us were trained to keep private things private. In other words, we don't air our dirty laundry publicly. It may be difficult to break this habit. In one study, almost three out of four people thought that if they brought up their sexual concerns, their doctor would not answer them[2]. Is it that the nurse practitioner may not think that their concerns are valid? Or is it that the physician assistant feels that these problems are normal after menopause? Could it be that since it is hard to get compensation, there is little incentive to treat patients with these issues? In terms of embarrassment, I will tell you that almost anything that you have a question about has already been asked of me. I can offer help but I have to hear about the situation first. Doctors can't mind read, at least not this one.

1.6 What kind of doctor deals with sexual problems?

Generally, your first contact should be your primary care provider. They may have the expertise to help you or they will refer you to a more appropriate practitioner. This may be a gynecologist like me or a psychologist, urologist, psychiatrist, geriatrician, etc. In addition, some patients prefer a provider of their own gender, general age or ethnic background. These preferences also tend to change over time. Many times I have been told that I was a woman's first male gynecologist and though initially they were apprehensive, they find me to be more empathetic or gentle to their previous providers. Or commonly, they might say that in the beginning I looked too young but they got over that; that I am "OK". My take is that I guess that I am aging just like my patients! It is also important for you to tell your provider what your goals are. Practitioners sometimes assume what patients want; that may not always be the case. For example, Mrs. W, age 54 came in with low libido problems. "Doc, I just don't care about having sex." Instead of assuming that she wanted to increase her sex drive, I spent time discussing things with her. It turns out that her husband had just been diagnosed with kidney cancer in addition to his heart problems. She made it clear that she did not want to have more sex right now. It would not have been in her best interest to send her to the lab for hundreds of dollars of hormonal blood level testing. Rather she was telling me that there was a lot on her plate right now.

1.7 Why is sex important?

Good question. There are psychological and physiological benefits to having sex. One study presented by Dr. S. Ebrahim, Ph.D., showed a reduction by half in heart disease when people were sexually active. There may even be a life extension benefit; we should see more information on this in the upcoming years. The Queens University in Belfast found that in 1,000 middle-aged men tracked over ten years, the men who had the most orgasms had half the mortality of the control group of men. Sex may reduce the incidence of depression, viral colds as well as weight gain. The British Journal of Urology International reported that even 20 year olds can reduce their chances of prostate cancer by ejaculating five times a week. Studies show that women who remain sexually active have less vaginal atrophy and higher testosterone levels.

As we age, we find that sex becomes less of a physical exercise. Patients report to me that the sexual act becomes more a way to get close to someone. It involves a lot of trust. Sex can be comforting both physically and emotionally and it plays an important part in relationships. People do not lose the need for love and intimacy as they age. Unfortunately when folks experience a sexual problem, they tend not to resume sexual activities. This is typically more common in men.

The majority of people feel that a healthy interest in sex is a critical part of a functioning relationship.

1.8 I've heard that sex is better with age. I'm not sure if I believe it. Is this true?

There definitely seems to be a large number of seniors who agree with this statement. I hear this over and over again in my office. For starters, there is no fear of pregnancy. Even my patients who had infertility issues in their younger years come to grips with the realization that they will not have any or more children. This has the benefit of allowing sexual activities to be enjoyed without worrying about ovulation timing and trips to the doctor's office. There is also a maturity to sex that was not present before. You have all those years of experience to tap into. The kids are out of the house (generally!) which gives folks more privacy to enjoy each other's company. No more sneaking around. Financially, many seniors are out of the rat race so even if they are on a fixed income, there isn't the hectic work schedule. Sex can happen at all times of the day rather than just in the evening or on weekends. Instead of trying to fit in sex between soccer games and school meetings, you can take all the time that you need or want. How many times have I heard that older patients would not go back to an earlier time if they had the choice? Many would not want much younger partners either, mainly stating that they didn't want to have to "train" them! As we age, sex can be more of a method of communication. Often, we can express ourselves more during sex. I think that we gain self confidence with age and feel more comfortable acknowledging our likes and dislikes. Sex can be joyous. How many teenagers describe sex that way?

1.9 What is a senior?

By definition a senior can be anyone older than you. There are seniors in high school and college as well as in business. The definition "someone advanced in years" also comes up but that can be somewhat non-specific. In some housing communities, seniors are 50 or more years old. Or 55 or 60…. So, what do I mean by senior? Basically, anyone who feels like a senior or fits one of the standard definitions. These are the folks who I feel can get the most benefit from reading this book. And there are a lot of you out there! This era in human life expectancy is unprecedented. For example the average person lived to 27 in 1700, 27 in 1800, 30 in 1900 and now 65 in the year 2000. There are many more seniors than ever before, and they live longer and healthier.

1.10 What are the stats?

On the last US Census estimates, we see that the median age has consistently increased over time. In the United States, the average age is 37.6 years old. We are getting older as a country. There are over 8 million 70-74 year olds, 7 million 75-79 year olds, 5 million 80-84 year olds, 3 million 85-89 year olds, 1 million 90-94 year olds and over 400,000 95-99 year olds. The Census also showed that of the 70,104 100+ year olds, 80% are female. We also see that about 40% of women describe sexual problems[1] but this can go up almost to 90% after menopause.[3]

1.11 Why don't doctors discuss sexual issues?

I can't respond to your individual doctor's reticence however I have heard and observed a number of reasons: the doctor is too busy to discuss anything but what was written on the chart, she is not comfortable discussing sexuality in general, there is not enough training for doctors in this field, you, as the patient, do not ask specific questions.... All of the above can be actual problems but remember that a doctor can not read your mind, you may need to be assertive and direct with your questions. Bring in a list of things you would want covered. Start with the most important issues first so you can be sure to get the attention that you deserve.

1.12 Why are there so few resources for us?

Good question. Not sure. Is it that seniors have been ignored by mainstream researchers? I think that there is some truth to that. I have done extensive amount of clinical research over the years and most protocols are extremely specific and limiting. Many seniors take multiple medications and have medical issues that might interfere with the pharmaceutical that is being studied. It gets too complicated and expensive for the drug company to sort this out therefore they are not usually targeted for study. Most of my protocols have criteria which start with the exclusion of anyone over 50.

1.13 Why is this book written predominantly from a female perspective?

There are two main reasons for this. My entire professional career has been dedicated to women's health. From medical school onward, I have been trained by my teachers, as well as my patients, with women in mind. I am used to working with women and so this is an extension of my work.

Secondly, the world is becoming more feminine as we age. Quite honestly, the male population shrinks over time so more of the senior patients who we see in the clinic are female. I have not entirely ignored the second half. In these pages you will read about erectile problems, premature ejaculators and depression in men.

1.14 Who am I?

Daniel Laury. I have an AA, BA and a MD, and majored in Premedical studies, biology and chemistry. I am in private practice in southern Oregon. I am a fellow of the College of Obstetricians and Gynecologist. My brother, father, grandmother and grandfather are or were doctors. I have always been immersed in the medical field. While many kids grew up with cartoons and kids books, I read the Merck manual and Freud. That was all that was lying around the house. Shortly before finishing medical school at the Albert Einstein College of Medicine, I knew that I was going to go into women's health care. After about 15 years, I stopped delivering babies and my patient population instantly got older. I started talking about leakage of urine instead of amniotic fluid. I had more time now to get to know my patients. By listening to them, I learned what was important to them. As I talked to them, sexual functioning questions came up more frequently. Researching more in the field made me realize just how little information was available. I have written multiple articles for medical journals and given many talks. I produce a television program called "The Doctor is Listening" where people call or email in their questions for the show. My father has also written a book on sexuality "Comment Vivre Sa Sexualite" so I suppose that there are some genetics here. He actually had the title of "sexologist"!

1.15 How do I read this book?

I expect that there will be at least three kinds of readers. The "disciplined reader" will start at the beginning and end on the last page of the book. These folks will get the most out of this book. The "referential reader" will use it like a dictionary, looking up specific issues. They are likely to refer back to it over time as questions pop up or that they wanted to refresh their knowledge. And the "scanning reader", who I think will be the common type, will start on question 1.1 and skim through the pages until an item causes them to pause and read. In this way, they cover the entire book but only read questions that hold their interest. There is no right or wrong way to read this book. If you are like me, you find that textbooks don't maintain your attention very long. I wrote it in a question and answer format to sustain interest and to allow all three types of readers the opportunity to benefit from it. I have included a glossary and an index in the back of this book as well.

2
What is Normal?

2.1 What is old?

The National Coalition On Aging (NCOA)[4] found that "old" is defined by people as being 70 for males and 75 for females. Having said that, most respondents did not define old based on age, most defined it based on physical decline. They also felt that mental decline and retirement was similar in importance than being a specific age. In medicine, we talk about the old old and the young old. We all know seniors who are full of energy. They plan things, volunteer extensively, go to get togethers and generally enjoy life. We also know middle aged people who struggle to get through their day, always complaining about perceived hardships.

2.2 What is normal about aging?

In the NCOA study about 50% of seniors said that they had hypertension and 50% said that they had arthritis. About 90% of seniors said that having family and friends were keys to having a meaningful, vital life. Health was important in 90% of seniors, spirituality was important in 70%, but only 20% report that sexuality was important. Interestingly in the same study, at least 80% people felt that a 75 year old male and female could be sexy!

Getting older also means a change in roles. Typically you start as a child and a receiver of attention. Then, in the middle years, you are in the production phase (income, children…) and accumulate assets (home, cars, retirement funds…). In the senior years, the role reversal can be a difficult transition, going from dominant to subservient, from care giving to care receiving and from money maker to money user. Some people make the transition more smoothly than others.

2.3 What is sex?

Generally, I use the following definition: the stimulation of the genital organs. It is very important for the provider to understand what you mean when you talk about sex. For some of my patients, it means only vaginal intercourse. In their mind, anal or oral intercourse doesn't "count". In terms of my lesbian patients, I need to be extra clear as to what they describe as sex. Masturbation can be considered "sex" as well. So, you can see that though it is a basic question, the answer may not be so simple. I find that I need to clarify what my patients mean so I can help them appropriately and that involves asking specific questions about their practices which can be embarrassing to them. Here is where sensitivity is very important and I make it a point of acknowledging their difficulties.

2.4 Talk to me about orgasms.

Whew! Two hard questions in a row. Let's start with the standard description. Men and women go through many of the parts of the sexual response cycle in the same way.

The first phase is called desire. It is a feeling of having the interest in being sexual. This can occur through thoughts and fantasies, that is, by an internal process. Or it can be external, by responding to a partner's actions for example.

The next step is called arousal. There are physical and psychological responses to sexual stimulation. Typically in women, there is an increase in vaginal lubrication and length. The heart rate increases and the breasts, vaginal lips and clitoris get swollen. There is a rash that can occur and the nipples may get erect. Males achieve erection and the scrotal skin thickens and pulls the testicles closer to the body.

Plateau phase involves the maximal intensity of arousal. This is the phase before orgasm and there is a point at which having an orgasm becomes inevitable. Incidentally, there are potential problems that can occur in each phase which you can read about in the sexual disorder chapter.

Orgasm occurs when there is an intense muscular rhythmic set of contractions associated with a release of the sexual tension. The contractions can range from 3 to 15 spasms or contractions that tighten and release the pubococcygeus muscles. In women, the uterus may also contract if it is present. Now here is where the sexes diverge. Males go through a resolution phase where heart rate and breathing slows down, the penis becomes limp and there is some sweating and they have a refractory phase where another immediate orgasm is impossible. Women also lose the swelling but can potentially go on to have another orgasm right away.

In my many years of talking with my patients, very few women describe being consistently multiorgasmic. As an aside, those who can have multiple orgasms tend to lose that potential as they age. I generally agree with Dr. Alan Wabrek who states that an adequate sexual response requires "effective stimulation of a sufficient quantity in a nurturing environment."[6] If any of these three components are missing, it can lead to poor sexual functioning.

2.5 Why is it that so many of my friends say that intercourse never gives them an orgasm?

Let's first review the anatomy. In women, much of the stimulation that leads to orgasm occurs at the clitoris. The external genitals and lower 1/3 of the vagina have most of the sensation. So, with intercourse, often those important areas are not being directly stimulated. That is why relatively few women will have a spontaneous orgasm just with intercourse. I have seen numbers in the 30% range. Having said that, many will be able to have a climax if the clitoris is stimulated by herself or her partner during intercourse. This can be done by hand or by changing the sexual position so that area is being rubbed. Female superior position is probably better at getting these angles right. It is always amazing to me how many women think that they are abnormal in some fashion since they don't get an orgasm with intercourse. Bridge techniques are useful to give women intercourse orgasms (see question 3.2).

2.6 What is the deal with orgasm for each gender?

It is my professional opinion that males tend to be more orgasm oriented.

Women are more complicated. Sometimes they just enjoy the foreplay and intercourse part but don't require a climax. Orgasm is a nice plus but the making of love is the important thing. Other times, they can be very goal oriented, making sure that they get their orgasm. I know many women who are very satisfied with their sex life but never have an orgasm. Quoting my father: "to use a musical analogy, they have learned that the overture can be the most beautiful part of an opera."[5] Males, I would venture to say, prefer the finale. Studies have suggested that up to 87 percent of women are satisfied with their sex life. Orgasms/ejaculations in males are usually more obvious to both parties, though not always. Some men have such a small ejaculatory volume that it may be missed and some men have retrograde ejaculation where the semen goes into their bladders instead of outside of the body so no fluid may be seen. Men also go through a refractory period after orgasm where stimulation will not result in erection nor ejaculation. The time involved is variable but can as long as days as men mature. In women, orgasms can be multiple as there is no waiting period.

2.7 My friend wants me to take hormones to improve my sex life. Should I spend the money on these products?

There are many types of hormones. Some of the better known ones include estrogen and testosterone. Yes, it is important to have your hormones in optimal range however this does not guarantee normal sexual functioning. I have seen information that suggests sexual activity in females is related to hormones 45% of the time. This means that even if your hormones are perfectly within normal limits, you may or may not want to have sex. In males however, sex is 95% hormonal. So, if the hormones are off, sex just won't happen. When I deal with sexual problems in the office, I stress that treating sexual problems is much more complicated in women. Just give males an erection and everything is usually fine but there are a lot more issues at work in females. Obviously, that is an exaggeration but perhaps not by as much as you might think. That is why there is no little blue pill for women (yet). The bottom line is that having your hormones in the optimal range is good but may not fix the problem.

2.8 Are most sexual problems a male thing or a female thing?

Remember that a sexual relationship requires a partner. Think of it as a ballet. If one of the partners is off on their timing, the whole dance falls apart. There are specific problems associated with each gender but often I find that there are shared responsibilities. A typical scenario: Jamie, age 55, comes in and says "I don't enjoy sex." She sees the problem as her own however when we discuss the situation with Jerry, her 57 year old husband, we see the other side of the coin. He responds strongly to her nakedness. For example, when Jerry sees his wife toweling off after a shower, he responds in a sexual fashion and he approaches her for sex. From his perspective, he sees his wife naked and wants to have sex. From her perspective, she was just showering and happens to leave the bathroom door open. She was not trying to stimulate him nor was she intending to have intercourse with him.

Here we have a common problem. Fortunately, it is relatively easy to fix using the sensate focusing technique which I have adapted for my patients. Other common reasons for sexual dysfunctions include fatigue and timing. I'll discuss each separately in the following questions.

2.9 What is sensate focusing?

Originally, Masters and Johnson of sexual therapy fame described a technique which patterned the sensory appreciation in couples. In my version of their technique, I have both partners come in to the office. I establish that there is a problem between the partners and that both want improvement in the sexual relationship. I ask that they commit about six weeks to the therapy and that they follow it exactly as I describe. In effect, I propose a contract between all three of us. In a heterosexual relationship for example, I ask the male "At a minimum, how many times a week would you need to have sex." Generally, he will respond with "two." One to three times a week is OK also. In this example, for the first week, I ask that the woman allow her husband to have sex with her twice a week whether she wants it or not. Then, I ask that the husband give his wife a foot massage twice that week on different days than when intercourse occurs. So, for the first week, there will be two days of foot massages and two days of intercourse. If he gets sexually stimulated on the massage days he is instructed not to use his wife as an outlet. The second week is the same for the intercourse frequency but now, the husband will give his wife two back massages instead of the foot rubs. The third week might involve leg massage, etc. By the sixth week, the man is able to touch, see and smell his wife's body without responding by approaching her for sex. This often works wonderfully to help the woman feel comfortable with her activities around the man and helps the man dissociate the sex from the body. Previously, a woman with a headache might have been uncomfortable asking her partner for a neck massage because it would inevitably lead to sex (up to 70% of back rubs end up with sex). Now, the neck massage is separated from the lovemaking. It really works great when both parties follow the agreement.

2.10 What is the difference between older and younger people having sex?

I assume that you are not talking about the physical act but the idea. Looking at the media, it is clear that sexuality is emphasized in the younger population, at the expense of the older folks. There are plenty of movies, photographs and advertisements showing youthful actors and models engaging in sexual relationships but very few of the older group. In fact, it is often de-emphasized. Our society clearly promotes youthful beauty; leading us erroneously to believe that old is not attractive. Similarly, people tend to smile when they see young folks kissing in public yet there is a general feeling of unease when seniors do the same. The expression "Dirty Old Man" and "Young Love" is a lot more common than "Dirty Young Man" and "Old Love." What is going on here? How did this come about? One theory suggests that we are uncomfortable thinking about our parents as being sexual. This can generalize to any older adult. Another theory stems from the idea that sex is for making babies. If someone is past childbearing age then their sexuality should be retired. Finally, increasing age uncomfortably forces us to address our own mortality. If we ignore the older population, perhaps we will not be reminded of our finite existence.

Dr. Neal E. Cutler, Ph.D., NCOA's director of survey research said that "when older people are not sexually active, it is usually because they lack a partner or because they have a medical condition." He did not say that older folks were not interested in sex.

James Firman, Ph.D., president and CEO of NCOA summarized this nicely for us. "For many older Americans, sex remains an important and vital part of their lives."

To answer your question, there really is very little difference physically between people having sex at any age. There are, however, issues surrounding availability of partners, medical hurdles, societal pressures and psychological barriers that limit sexual activities with age.

2.11 What are the advantages to getting older?

This might surprise some readers but when I ask patients, the most common answer is "Dr. Laury, sex is better now." Almost invariably, my patients agree that getting older has its advantages and that includes sex. There is a lifetime's experience to tap into. Many of people's inhibitions particularly in regards to sexuality have been overcome. Commonly, patients describe sex in the teens and twenties as somewhat of a gymnastic experience: how long they did they last, where they did it, in what position, etc.). As people age, sex becomes more an expression of love, comfort and sharing. In addition, after menopause, there is no fear of pregnancy which may improve relations. Many of my younger patients have major stress dealing with this possibility. They lose sleep, they take the morning after pill, they have relationship issues because of the potential of an unwanted pregnancy. Forget all of that after menopause. Younger folks often have to work around menstrual bleeding. Though some people have sex during menses, they tend to be in the minority. After menopause, sex can occur at any time. A 2000 National Council on Aging (NCOA) study found that 90% of the elderly felt that they were satisfied with their life up until the time of the study. In addition, 45% felt that these were the best years of their life. When sexually active older people were more specifically queried about the emotional satisfaction they get from sex, 74% of men and 70% of women said they were at least as satisfied or more than they were in their 40s. In an AARP/Modern Maturity magazine survey in over 45 year olds done in 1999, they found that 67% of people with sexual partners were extremely or somewhat satisfied with their sex lives. Having said all of the above, I need to at least acknowledge the possibility of sadness after menopause because of the loss of fertility. This can be distressful to some people. Financially, there can also be advantages to aging. Student loans, mortgages, college costs are less common. So, over all, there are definite benefits to aging.

2.12 What are the disadvantages to getting older?

There is an entire book that could be written on the changes that occur with aging. Whether or not you consider these as negative really depends on your mindset. We know that in males, they tend to achieve less rigid erections. Males have also described requiring more stimulation to get that erection and, ultimately, ejaculate. The refractory period that we talked about in question 2.4 is also prolonged. Whereas a younger man might be able to get an erection within minutes of ejaculation, an older man might have to wait hours or even days.

Women are not immune to sexual changes either. Felt to be related to a reduction in estrogens, breasts lose tone and start heading south responding inexorably to the call of gravity. The vaginal lips tend to thin out and get smaller. The vagina itself loses elasticity and lubrication which can cause pain with intercourse. Clitoris size is reduced as is the sensitivity. The uterus tends to shrink which may sometimes be an advantage if a previously enlarged womb got in the way of sex or hurt with orgasm. As testosterone levels decrease, both sexes may notice a reduction in libido. Interestingly, the progress of many of these changes can be stopped or even reversed with certain medications and hormones. Sexual activity itself has been shown to help or maintain sexual functioning. There is an increase in bladder infections as well as vulvar and vaginal infections.

We know that sexual activity decreases as we age. In the NCOA sexual inventory study, 71% of men vs. 51% of women in their 60s were sexually active. In their 70s the numbers were 57% of men vs. 30% of women.

Yes, there are disadvantages to getting older but most folks appreciate the positive and deemphasize the negative. Mrs. G, age 68 summed it up "Getting old is not for wimps."

2.13 Is masturbation normal?

The short answer is yes. Self stimulation is not only limited to humans either. Many families have dogs who rub themselves at inopportune times on stuffed animals, shoes and even the family cat. Monkeys in zoos are famous for public masturbation. Solo sex, as I have seen it called, can be a reasonable substitute for sex with a partner when one is not available. It is also a reasonable activity when a partner is present. To quote Woody Allen "Don't knock masturbation - it's sex with someone I love".

Depending on which study you read 97% of men and 83% of women have self-stimulated at some time in their lives. The Kinsey Report from the 1950s found that 92% of men and 58% of women have masturbated. So, clearly it is common and normal. The problems that can occur include psychological anxiety associated with masturbation as well as the excessive or exclusive use of that sexual stimulation rather than partner sex. If someone masturbates to the exclusion of their partner, I would say that there is a problem with the relationship. If someone gets into legal difficulties because of over self-stimulation, then, there too, there is a problem. I have also seen physical trauma from excessive masturbation. One of my patients has a thickened, enlarged clitoris because of too much rubbing. To be somewhat simplistic, normal masturbation is normal and abnormal is not. Interestingly, when there is a strong conviction against masturbation (religious, personal…) people can sometimes convert that sexual energy into something else. The process, called sublimation, can be seen when folks pour all this energy into sports or writing as examples. Masturbation can bring sexual tension relief, it can help with pain, it can keep the pelvic organs functioning and it can help people sleep. In some studies, there is an association where the higher the number of ejaculations, the lower the prostate cancer risk. One theory is that ejaculation clears out chemicals that can cause cancer. Most people usually figure out how to masturbate by exploring what feels good to them, however a fair number of people have had "mentors" to help them. There are even classes available if needed.

2.14 How normal is homosexuality?

Historically, homosexual activities have always been described. No matter how repressed or restrictive the era, there has been lesbian and gay sex. In a recent US survey, there were 4,300,000 people who described themselves as gay, lesbian, bisexual or transsexual (GLBT), which means that 1.51% of the population is GLBT. Of those, 900,000 are lesbian and 2,000,000 are gay men. In another study, 1.3% of women have had a same sex partner in the last year. According to the American Psychological Association Guideline #1 for dealing with the Gay and Lesbian population: "Psychologists understand that homosexuality and bisexuality are not indicative of mental illness." So there you have it. Interestingly, it is felt that being gay or lesbian is a result of complex interplay of genetics, biochemistry and environment. It is not subject to a conscious decision to be homosexual. It is also inappropriate to try to reassign sexual orientation. People don't decide to be gay or lesbian; it is part of their sexual makeup. Their orientation can change over time as well, for example, the majority of lesbians have had sex with a male.

2.15 How many times a week is normal?

Remember that normal or average is usually a range for most human experiences. How many women do you personally know who actually have 1.83 babies (according to the National Center of Health Statistics, 2002) and owns 0.87 televisions (Natural Resources Defense Council, Televisions: Active Mode Energy Use, New Horizons for Energy Efficiency, March 2005. p. 3)? Yet those are the averages. Approximately three percent of women have never had sexual intercourse in their life on one end of the spectrum. From the other side, seven percent have it four or more times a week[1]. Everyone falls somewhere in between. From personal interviews over many years, I find that an "average" couple has sex twice a week. The frequency falls off during menstruation, during pregnancy and after having children. Thursday's and Sunday's are the most common days to have sex. In the National Council on the Aging (NCOA) study, 52% of people over 60 have sex less than once a month, leaving almost half having sexual activity more than once a month. However, 54% of these men and 26% of the women said they would prefer to have sexual activities more often. In this study, folks also reported that vaginal intercourse was the most enjoyable. They also liked giving and receiving oral sex as well as watching their partner undress. Thirty nine percent of those queried said that they were satisfied with the amount of sex they currently have. Another 39% would prefer more sex and only 4% said that they wanted less.

Couples like Mr. and Mrs. M. are common. Mr. M would like to have sex three times a week but his wife prefers once or twice a month. We try to figure out what issues are at work here. Does she have pain with sex, is he being disrespectful to her, is she having an affair, is he depressed…?

The bottom line is that "normal" really has to do with you and your partner's desires not what is nationally recognized as average.

2.16 This may seem like a stupid question but what is the difference between men and women?

As many of you embryologists are aware, we all start out as female. Testosterone then influences the growing organs in 50% of fetuses to make them look and act male. This "boy" hormone is responsible for all of the obvious external differences. It also works on the inside structures including the brain. This is important because there are true differences that can be found between women and men even in the way we speak, think and act. Studies have shown that women are more voluble; they speak much more than men. But do women communicate better than men? Are women's verbal skills more developed? Are men more efficient in their speech? Do all men have a feminine side and vice versa? Do artists think differently then other professionals? All are good questions but we don't have all the answers.

Other differences in brain functioning lead males to take more physical risks and women to be more loyal. This may be related to Testosterone and Oxytocin levels and there is a lot of research being done on them right now. Stay tuned. There may ultimately be a nasal spray that keeps your man from leaving the nest. What all of this means is that we should remember that we have two genders that interpret and act upon the environment differently. From a sexual point of view this is critical to keep in mind to help both genders through one of the most intimate and self-revealing of human experiences.

2.17 Help me Dr. Laury! My clitoris is disappearing. What is up with that?

Normally, the clitoris does change size depending on blood flow and under the influence of hormones and stimulation. Clitoromegaly describes a condition where the organ is much larger than normal. It can be seen with certain hormone abnormalities, especially excess testosterone and adrenal hyperplasias. There are also some tumors associated with it as well. Local stimulation can also swell that area. Clitoromegaly is usually a cosmetic issue once the abnormalities are corrected.

From the other end of the spectrum, we know that as women age, there tends to be a reduction in hormone levels that affect the vaginal tissues including the clitoris. Recently, we talked to a lady who is progressively having more problems having an orgasm with appropriate stimulation. The vaginal exam showed that her clitoris was quite small and had retracted under the clitoral hood. In addition, her labia minora were tiny. This suggested a lack of estrogen effect and so I would anticipate that with the appropriate replacement she should do fine. I will note that for this lady, I used vaginal estrogens as it will tend to work faster for her.

Some of my patients have bought an Eros Therapy system. Basically, it applies suction to the clitoris to increase sensitivity and size. They run about $400 and you need a prescription. I have not heard much feedback from these ladies but it did get FDA approval which shows that there is a positive effect.

You will also see advertised various creams. Some may increase sensitivity, others are irritants and can cause pain and a few are associated with allergic type responses. If you try some of these products, you may want to start low and go slow. I have heard about menthols, capsaicin and L-Arginine in some of them. Remember that you are essentially self-experimenting with these products.

There are other cases when the clitoris is not actually smaller but rather it is hidden behind the hood of the clitoris. Lichen sclerosis is the most common reason that I find for a hidden clitoris. This is a condition where the vagina progressively seals itself together (see question 8.2).

2.18 "Is it normal to like kissing more than sex?"

A 75 year old. Kissing is often a prelude to sex but can be erotic in its own right. Remember many years ago when you were just starting out sexually? Kissing was probably much more exciting than actually having sex? Most women's first intercourse experiences were less than stellar and may have actually been painful, embarrassing or subject to all sorts of psychological stressors. Kissing gets into personal space more than sex, oral included. The face is the site for more senses than another place on the body and your are, by definition, really face to face. A few pointers: poor dental hygiene can cause bad breath, smoker's mouth is a turn-off, dentures can move at inopportune times, out of practice tongues get tired quickly. Garlic and the onion family produce chemicals that are excreted through the lungs so they are harder to mask just with mints and brushing. Some people scrape their tongue as well. Another benefit of aging is that we lose many of our taste buds over time so we may tolerate some off tastes more. Many people feel that kissing is more stimulating than sex so you are in good company. Enjoy!

3
When Sex Doesn't Work...

3.1 Dr. Laury, I don't enjoy sex. What is going on?

This question and all of its variants come up daily in my practice. I could write a book on this question alone as about 43% of women aged 18-59 and probably a much higher percentage over 60 have a sexual dysfunction. About a third of women describe decreased sex drive. In my practice, it is higher than that probably because women know to come to our office with these problems. It is important to separate someone who has never enjoyed sex and one who has previously enjoyed it. Let's talk about the various possibilities and treatment options.

There are many different classifications of sexual disorders. A newer set of definitions as proposed by the AUA Foundation include the classic sexual desire and sexual arousal disorders. Then they split the arousal disorder into subjective and genital type abnormality. The first type describes the lack of sexual feelings or excitement that normally are present when stimulated sexually. In the second type, there are no actual physical changes that occur when stimulated sexually (e.g. no vaginal lubrication…). Interestingly, there is even a disorder that is described as the persistence of sexual arousal when there is no stimulation.

We know that sexual desire and sexual frequency decreases

with age. While this is considered a normal result of aging, there may many reasons why this may be occurring abnormally. Of the Sexual Disorders, the lack of interest in sex is the most common problem. Unfortunately, it may also be the hardest to treat.

The Hypoactive Sexual Desire Disorder (HSDD) means just that; the interest in engaging in sex is less than normal. Once sexual activity starts however these folks will generally respond normally. Women will commonly tell me that they could happily live the rest of their life without sex. They may go out of their way to avoid sex. Classic tricks include going to the bedroom at different times than their partner, pretending to be asleep, doing lots of other stuff around the house to stay busy when their partner is in the mood, etc. Many of these women will end up having sex out of the feeling of obligation to their partners. Typically, they say things like "He is a man and he needs it" or "I'm his wife and it is part of my duty". This leads to a poor relationship since they may fake enthusiasm and their partner ultimately figures this out.

Mrs. S has a fairly typical story. She came in yesterday to check on some labs (hormones and cholesterol levels) and mentioned that she has no interest in sex. Upon further discuss she tells me that this goes back two years. She is confused because she loves her husband, she has no sex pain, she responds normally to sexual stimulation and she is otherwise happy. The problem is that she has no interest in starting the process of sex. Her husband is understandably concerned and feels that it is his fault and he is starting to become more insecure. He has increased his attempts to get his wife "into the mood" and when they do have intercourse he spends extra time trying to please his wife.

I had to first figure out the cause that may have started this problem. Some of the more common issues that come up are, and in no special order:

1. Fatigue. As a rule, we are overtired. As we age, our sleep quality decreases. We wake up more through the night and don't feel as refreshed in the morning. When a partner tries to snuggle, the other one needs to make a decision. Sleep or sex? And most of the time, sleep is more important. For these folks, I often recommend setting a time for sex. For example, if hubby typically gets interested after dark, then try something in the morning. Go out on a date and then rent a hotel room. Fatigue is also more common as we age in response to surgery. When the doctor says that it will take only a few weeks to recuperate, that may be an average for younger patients. It can take up to a year for an older person to feel back to normal after major surgery.

2. Sex pain. More about that later in this chapter (4.3)

3. Interpersonal issues. See chapter 7

4. Patterned response. I addressed this in question 2.9, but it pays to repeat some of that information. Often males respond sexually to a situation that was not intended to be sexual. Say a woman is getting out of the shower and is drying off. Seeing her naked may stimulate him who then approaches her for sex yet her intent was just to get towelled off. She ultimately learns to close the bathroom door because of this response. Similarly, if she had a long day and her shoulders are tight, she might ask for a neck or back rub. About two thirds of the time, this will result in sex so she would rather got to bed with a neck ache rather than "risk" setting off this behavior pattern. This specific dysfunction is very fixable in my opinion.

5. Depression. Clearly anhedonism or the loss of interest in things is very much associated with depression. So if someone complains of a lack of libido, I feel that it is important to at least

consider this as a possibility. Depression is a treatable disease. Ignoring depression can be fatal in up to about 15% (suicide for example). Get in to a provider for this; do not try to treat this at home by yourself.

6. Medication side effects. Many pharmaceuticals can affect the libido either directly or indirectly. These include the SSRIs like Prozac, Paxil, Luvox, and Zoloft among others. Cardiac medications can also be implicated. Chapter Eight goes much more into depth.

3.2 I don't get an orgasm easily. What is the deal here?

Anorgasmia which simply means that there is no orgasm is fairly common. Up to 10% of women have never had an orgasm. In my practice, it is less than that but the fact remains that many people have never experienced climax. Other folks only experience it with certain sexual techniques (manual stimulation for example and not with intercourse). Rarely, people experience orgasm but don't recognize it as such. Anorgasmia has two flavors; primary and secondary. In primary, they have never had one. I find that this is the hardest one to treat because we don't know if they are even capable of having an orgasm and there is no history and experience to turn to. Often through discussion, a supportive partner or masturbation, people are able to achieve orgasm which can later on be bridged to other sexual techniques. The usual way that I help women achieve intercourse orgasms involved having her or her partner stimulate her while she is having sex. This may be manually or with a vibrator generally over the clitoral region. Over time, she will no longer need that additional stimulation to achieve an orgasm with intercourse. Even though I don't recommend alcohol to my patients, if they already drink, this can sometimes help; mainly through disinhibition.

Secondary anorgasmia means that orgasm used to be possible but not now. We try to find out reasons why this is no longer working. Is there pain? Are there marital issues? Is there fear involved? Do you need more stimulation? Also keep in mind that hardening of the arteries can lead to less blood flow to the pelvis. This can be associated with less intense orgasms for both genders.

3.3 Why does sex hurt?

Intercourse can be painful for either partner. Males can get poked by IUD (intrauterine device) strings if they are too short. If the IUD shifts, male intercourse pain may be the first suggestion that something is wrong. They can have painful orgasms, painful erections, infections, etc. In women, I find that there are many more possibilities for discomfort. The technical word for painful sex is dyspareunia. Some different types include introital dyspareunia (pain just with getting in the vagina), thrust dyspareunia (with penetration) and deep dyspareunia. Thinking about the female anatomy, we can see that penetration can be painful if the tissues are fragile as is common with estrogen loss. If the partner is too aggressive, there can also be tearing and frictional pain. The vagina can be very accommodating but it will take time and lubrication. Vaginismus occurs when the muscles just inside the vagina are very tight. These spasm and prevent or at least limit the ability to have sex because of the pain. Often there is a history of sexual abuse or trauma to the pelvis. I like to use the following analogy to explain things to my patients. "Think of your vagina like its own little person. If you treat it nice, it will let things in.

Previously, something has caused it pain so now whenever there is the threat of penetration (by finger, penis, speculum…) it shuts down. If you go slow, use lubrication and do some fairly simple exercises, eventually it will calm down and relax." There are two main exercises that I talk about. When there is just some excessive tightness, I show the woman how to put a finger in the vagina and push down towards the rectum. First I do that so she gets the feeling of how much pressure to use. Then I have her do the same thing before intercourse. She can also allow her partner to do this instead. When there is more serious vaginismus, she must first learn to get into the vagina with something very small. You can buy vaginal dilators in various sizes but one of the simplest and cheapest is to ask your provider for various sized syringe covers. These are shaped appropriately, should be free and are easy to clean. Then once she is able to get the smallest size in without pain, she can work her way up at her own pace.

Surgical and radiation changes can cause scarring and overtightening of the vagina. This can often be improved by liberal use of lubricants and working diligently at dilating the vagina. The most common surgeries that I hear about causing pain are the A & P repairs ("bladder tucks, rectocele repairs, vaginal surgeries, incontinence procedures"…). Poorly healed repairs after birth are the second most common scarring problem that I see. Episiotomies can cause painful scars but tears can do the same thing. Vulvar and vaginal cancer surgeries can lead to tightening of tissues.

Vaginal infections can also lead to painful sex. Once we figure out which type of infection is going on, we can start treatment which generally improve sexual functioning. Yeast vaginitis (Candida) is very common in women. Typically, there is itching, whitish curd-like discharge and vaginal pain. An abnormal odor is sometimes part of the presentation. As most of you know, there are many treatments available over-the-counter. Unfortunately, studies clearly show that many times the woman misdiagnoses the infection and therefore treats unsuccessfully with the wrong medication. In addition, even when the correct diagnosis is made, there is a high resistance to the over-the-counter antiyeast meds. We are now seeing more and more yeast infections that need to be treated with stronger meds. In the office setting, I do a visual check, vaginal pH, microscopic exam and a few chemical tests to confirm a diagnosis.

Deep dyspareunia is more a challenge for me as there are so many possibilities. Essentially, something is being bumped by the penis. My goal is figure out what is causing the pain and how to improve on it. Endometriosis can cause scarring in the pelvis often causing this pain. Ovarian cysts, prolapse of the pelvic organs, fibroid tumors, scar tissue, bladder infections, interstitial cystitis, etc. must also be considered. During the pelvic exam, I push on the different areas with my fingers attempting to gently reproduce her discomfort. Depending on the area that she responds to I can sometimes tell what the problem is. Laparoscopy (Belly button surgery using lighted tubes and instruments), ultrasound, CT scans and other imaging technologies can be helpful. Once we find the cause it is easier to fix things.

Sex can also hurt in certain positions and not in others. In my experience, women with a retroverted (back facing) uterus more commonly report that doggy style intercourse is more painful than missionary position. This is because the uterus is in direct line to being hit by her partner's thrusting. Sometimes the best option is simply to change positions. For these women, I have had lots of success asking them to use the female superior position where she can control depth and angle of penetration. Sometimes a partner is too heavy for a woman and this will cause pain (a lady today told me that he caused her to have reflux or heartburn when he lays on top of her). An abdominal surgical scar can also cause pain, particularly early on. Side to side sex can be helpful here. Back pain can interfere with sex for both partners. Some couples use special pillows, others have sex in the hot tub. Try something different!

3.4 I keep on getting yeast infections. Is my partner giving them back to me?

While this is possible, it is unusual. I usually say that in about 10% of the time, recurrent vaginal yeast infections are from reinfection from the male partner. Certain males have risk factors such as Diabetes and being uncircumcised. I will sometimes suggest treatment of a partner if we have too many recurrences. A trick that I use to treat men empirically is as follows. When I have a woman who I feel might be getting reinfected, I give her a good antiyeast vaginal cream. Then I advise her to have intercourse with her partner while there is still some cream inside her. This in effect treats both partners and has been very useful in my practice. Most males, I would think, otherwise might not be comfortable smearing cream all over their genitals. Other tricks that can sometimes help include making sure that your underwear has a cotton crotch. Synthetics may keep too much moisture in the vaginal area leading to yeast infections. Wet bathing suits are a common problem for some women. There is some thought that yeast spores can survive a round of hot water and detergent in the washing machine. Rarely, I have recommended that ladies microwave their panties to sterilize them. Usually, these ladies decline, and use that as an excuse to buy new ones.

3.5 I was told that I have vestibulitis. What is that?

Vestibulitis is a complex disorder. We are not sure what actually is the problem. Various theories are bantered around in medical circles. These include accumulation of various toxins in the vaginal tissues, response to viruses, fungi and bacteria, sexual abuse residual, etc. In terms of symptoms, usually these ladies come in with vaginal pain and burning of long duration. Intercourse can be painful or impossible to complete. I usually can come to the diagnosis rapidly during the exam. I simply touch the various areas just inside and outside of the vagina with a cotton tipped swab. If there is excessive pain, I am usually comfortable with calling her problem vestibulitis. Treatment is controversial since there are many different options. Sometimes various creams and soaks help, other times injections can be of benefit. When all else fails, surgery can be considered to remove the affected area.

3.6 Sex hurts and my doctor thinks that it is a lack of estrogen. What should I do?

The vagina is an organ that is very sensitive to estrogen levels. When there is not enough of that hormone, the tissues get less elastic and lubricate poorly leading to painful sex. In addition, women also commonly report a yellow vaginal discharge and/or vaginal dryness. Orgasm may become less intense or even painful. Low estrogen levels also affects the bone, breast and skin among other organs. We can see osteoporosis, sagging breasts and crinkly skin when the balance is upset.

Obviously, one option is to treat with estrogens. Depending on your history and wishes, estrogen therapy can be given locally (vaginal or skin creams) or systemically (pills, patches…). However not every woman may be able to or want to use estrogen. There is so much scary information as well as misinformation out there that some women just refuse all estrogen products. Therefore, I talk to ladies about vaginal lubricants. There are water and silicon based products out there. There are sprays, liquids and suppositories. I would recommend buying a few products and see which works better for you. Interestingly, sexual activities also help. It is the use it or lose it idea here. The theory is that sexual stimulation increases blood flow to the vagina which helps most of the above complaints.

3.7 I was told to go to counseling. How is this going to help with sex?

Counseling can be of great benefit for a variety of reasons. One example is when someone has anxiety about a relationship. Just yesterday, I saw a young woman who is torn between her sexual needs and her religious beliefs. We discussed how this can impact on her relationship. Very often women come in feeling "abnormal" because they don't orgasm with vaginal intercourse. After some education, they learn that this is very common and probably normal (at least initially. To read more about the bridge technique see question 3.2). Counseling can change a person's expectations as well as their perspective. When a man tells me that his wife doesn't want to have sex often it turns out that she actually does but not at the frequency or at the time and place that he wants it. By addressing the situation, he can see things from her perspective. Having a sexual relationship requires at least two consenting parties. Counseling has been of great help for some of my ladies who have been traumatized in the past through sexual abuse and rape. With about 22% of women admitting to being abused, it is no wonder that there is some much that therapy can help. The hardest part for me as a physician is to get my patients to accept the need for therapy. Then, I need to find an empathic and competent therapist. Finally, the therapy may not be covered by insurance, which limits the enthusiasm of my patients.

3.8 Dr. Laury, talk to me about spectatoring. I read about this in a woman's magazine but don't really understand it.

Many women self-modulate during sex. What I mean by that is that they are constantly evaluating their performance, their response and their appearance. It almost seems that they are outside of their body, taking notes for an imaginary article that they are about to write! The problem with spectatoring is that they can feel inhibited as when they worry about the way they look which can limit their enjoyment. They also are outside of the love making experience. We need to get them back in bed rather than sitting next to themselves evaluating the process. One of the best techniques to deal with spectatoring is directed masturbation. This brings back the focus which later can be bridged to sex with a partner. Counseling can also be very helpful here. Self-confidence issues generally surface during the sessions. A slightly different type which I call secondary spectatoring involves treatment of sexual dysfunction. Let's say that Fran, age 67 comes in with the following story. "I might be planning to become sexual with someone soon however it has been 24 years since I have done anything like this. Will I be able to have sex?" We talk about STIs, previous issues, goals, etc. During the exam, I note some vaginal tightness and dryness. I instruct her on vaginal stretches and lubrication. If and when sex occurs, Fran now starts going over my instructions. It can seem to her that I am mentally standing by her bedside coaching her through the process. That is certainly not the most conducive way to enjoy the moment.

3.9 What is the difference between low sex drive that is generalized or that is selective or specific?

Generalized low sex drive is associated with depression, fatigue, hormone imbalances and poor self-confidence. When someone is depressed, sexual interest is very often lacking. When I go through the criteria with my patients and ask about sexual interest, I often hear from them: "I wouldn't care if I never have sex ever again" and "Sex? Take it or leave it. I would rather sleep." As the depression lifts, we often see libido improve. Certain medications that we use for depression, anxiety, panic disorder and Obsessive/Compulsive Disorder (OCD) as examples can have a negative impact on sexual functioning. Commonly, they prolong the plateau phase (see question 2.4) which makes it more difficult to achieve an orgasm. This, in turn, can frustrate folks so they end up having less sex. It is difficult, on occasion, for us to document improvement in the depression because of this side effect.

When someone tells me that they don't want to have sex with their partner but still has fantasies, this usually suggests a relationship situation rather than a sexual desire problem. Empathetic counseling will help bring some of these issues to the surface for discussion. There is also the possibility that there is a lack of sexual attraction to their partner. People change physically over time and also, after surgery, rather rapidly. Sometimes this can cause a lack of desire. A good example is after colon cancer surgery when a colostomy bag may be necessary. This can be unattractive to both partners leading to less sexual desire. Unfortunately, after a couple stops having intercourse, it becomes harder and harder to resume the longer they wait. So even if the colostomy is "taken down" and reversed, we can still see sexual disorders. I always try to figure out if the low libido is generalized or specific as it may very well point me to a different treatment option.

    Let's talk more about body issues. People develop various skin issues as they age. Commonly, there are small red bumps (hemangiomata), raised grey to black rough patches (seborrheic keratoses), eczema, psoriasis, skin cancers, etc. Some folks worry about catching or transmitting dermal diseases to their partner. Indeed, some skin abnormalities can be spread through contact such as molluscum contagiosum but many can not. I would recommend that you see your provider to get an accurate diagnosis and ask them if it is contagious.

    There is also a concern about embarrassment with certain sexual disorders. Here is another example where age is of benefit. Often I find my younger patients are more concerned about others seeing their body in the nude. Over time, I also find that they learn that there is a time and place for modesty. That modesty usually is relaxed when they are sexually active. I rarely hear of my older patients requiring the lights be off when they make love. However, since their body is more visible, some people may be concerned about looking attractive to themselves or their partners. I usually help them through this issue by asking the partner if they find them attractive. Generally, the answer is yes which may reassure the individual.

Don't assume things. Communicate with your partner. Indeed there are changes as we age, but love making matures with age; it is more than just a pretty body that we seek. I find it important to separate the self loathing from the partner's disinterest. Some of the things that you can do to improve the way you look include stopping smoking, try to get to an ideal body weight and exercise more. There are many cosmetic procedures that are available as well. Tummy tucks and breast lifts to Intense Pulsed Light Photorejuvenation (IPL) and dermal fillers. This is a very exciting time in the cosmetic field. We are working with hair regrowth techniques, blue light reversal of skin aging, radiofrequency skin tightening, cellulite lasers… It is important to feel good about yourself however I would encourage people to think about why they want to have certain procedures done. What is the motivation? To cheat age? To look good for yourself? Your partner?

What about breast cancer, sex and mastectomies? Though the female breast is an obvious sexual organ and inexorably linked to being a woman, most women who have had either lumpectomies or mastectomies do not have any sexual dysfunction after the procedure. For some, breasts are simply milk producing organs that have no use after childbearing. These women tell me that if they could "chop them off" that would be just fine. They were useful previously but now just contribute to back and neck pain. Furthermore, they are a setup for cancer.

For others, breasts are very much a symbol of their femininity. It is what clearly differentiates them from males visually. Breastfeeding is strictly a woman's prerogative. After surgery, we often recommend implants or prostheses so the loss of one or both breasts is not so obvious to the casual observer. Sexual touching and looking at the surgically altered chest and breast may be reduced after procedures. Sensation at the surgical site can be altered. There may be embarrassment issues as well. The woman's presurgical sexual functioning, her psychological health and the personal relationship with her partner are all very important indicators of her adaptability after mastectomy.[4]

3.10 Is it wrong to fake an orgasm?

I am not sure what the word "wrong" means. Think about why you feel the need to fake it. Are you trying to get sex over with earlier? Are you trying to make your partner feel that they have succeeded in pleasuring you? Are you trying to impress the neighbors? Once you figure out why you would consider faking it, you can decide if it is worth the acting. Though it is generally accepted that males can't fake orgasm, there is some information available that suggests that there is a difference between orgasm and ejaculation. Hopefully, we'll hear more about this as more studies are done. Both males and females have admitted to faking orgasms so you are not alone.

3.11 My wife has ovary cancer. Will I catch it if I have sex with her?

Cancer generates intense fears, some of which are unfounded. Breast cancer is not contagious, neither is ovarian or uterine. Cervical cancer is a bit more complicated. Yes, we think that viruses are necessary to start the process towards cervical cancer. In general, these are transmitted sexually. However, treated cervical cancer is not going to spread. And in addition, having sex will not make the cancer come back. Often, we see that sexuality after dealing with a cancer may be affected. Let's say that your wife survived a bout with breast cancer. During the treatment she lost a breast to surgery. She or you may be uncomfortable seeing the resultant scar. Or the area may be painful to touch. Depression is commonly seen when dealing with cancer. A lack of sexual desire is associated with depression so it would not be surprising to hear that the partner with cancer is not interested in sex. Even if they are not depressed, the treatment can be grueling which puts sex on the back burner. Who wants to have sex when they are nauseated or excessively tired? Cancer survivors have mentioned to me that sometimes instead of sex, they just want to be held. Communication is key for both folks.

3.12 Please tell me how to make sex more exciting.

First let's explore why sex may not be that exciting to you. There are many reasons why I see folks complain of sexual disinterest. Sexual boredom can occur, typically when couples have too strict of patterns. For example, the average American couple has sex twice a week. Usually Thursday and Sunday, in case you are interested in that specific information. So, if you know that you are likely to have your few minutes of intercourse every Thursday, then it can easily become boring. If your partner always uses the same technique, that too can be a problem.

Often, it helps to change up your pattern. Try to go out on a date for example. Experiment with different clothes, techniques and positions. Communicate with your sexual partner, explain what works for you and what doesn't. Let them in on your fantasies. Use audiovisual aids like DVDs or provocative magazines. In other words, be creative. Don't let sex become unexciting. Don't expect too much from sex but also, don't expect too little.

For some women, doing the Kegel exercises during intercourse helps as well. These muscles tighten and lift the vaginal tissues and may be useful in increasing sexual satisfaction for both parties.

When I see a patient with a lack of sexual interest, the most important question that I have is how this compares to her previous interest. Some people have always had low libido and some have lost some of it more recently. I use a number of different treatment options depending on the cause. Psychological counseling, changing of medications, sensate focusing, estrogen therapy, etc. have all proved to be useful in my practice.

3.13 I used to always have orgasms with intercourse. Now it is a lot more work. What is going on?

There are many possibilities, some of which we previously addressed. Orgasm requires a supportive environment with adequate stimulation. If the tissues are lacking estrogens, they may feel raw or irritated instead of pleasurably stimulated. In addition, up to about 50% of women won't have an orgasm with sex, though it sounds like this used to be possible for you. I would recommend spending more time with the foreplay and use plenty of lubricant. If this doesn't help, consider asking your provider if estrogen is right for you. Clearly, there are more potential issues here that need to be identified. How is the relationship? Is the quality of his erection the same as before? Are there other concerns that interfere with your intimacy? Many couples have learned to give the woman an orgasm first then proceed to intercourse. The bridge technique described more fully in question 3.2, may be helpful to relink intercourse with orgasm.

3.14 I was told that I have HSDD, can you explain that to me?

Hypoactive Sexual Desire Disorder is fairly common and probably under-recognized. It is generally used to describe people who respond normally to sexual stimulation but do not have the desire to initiate or become sexually active. Among the sexual desire disorders, researchers have found that about a third of women lacked interest in sex, 30% had orgasm issues, 20% found sex not to be pleasurable, 20% had problems adequately lubricating and 15% had pain with sex.[1]

There are some very good ways of improving or fixing many of these problems. It really depends on the problem and how motivated the patient is. As an aside, there is much research now being focused on just this problem. We'll have to wait and see what becomes available.

3.15 OK Dr. Laury, I now realize that I have a problem. What is the next step?

Congratulations! Just by educating yourself, you have made the first movement towards improving your situation. I would recommend that you find a competent and caring provider that has the appropriate credentials. There are plenty of folks who mean well but don't have the training and experience to help. Often patients come to me after allowing their friends or a free "counselor" to try and help them. For many sexual difficulties an exam is critical. We may find anatomic abnormalities like effects of low estrogens, or sometimes even cancer. It is not fair to you to assume that the problem is in your head if there are physical reasons for your symptoms. Also, let your provider know if you have or are still using alternative treatment options. I like to hear about herbal preparations, vitamins, acupuncture, biofeedback, hypnosis, etc. This tells me what works and what doesn't for you. By reading this book, it is clear to me that you are interested in enhancing yourself.

3.16 I've had a hysterectomy and now sex feels different. What is wrong with me?

There are many reasons why your complaint is a common one. Typically, my patients mention that there are sexual changes after hysterectomy. You didn't mention if your ovaries were removed at the time of hysterectomy. If so, there was an abrupt reduction in the ovary hormones. This can lead to hot flashes and vaginal dryness within a few days of surgery. Even if the ovaries were left in place, we still hear of transient hormone changes. I think that the reason for this is that anatomically, the ovaries get about a third of their blood supply from the uterus side. When the uterus is removed, there is a sudden drop in circulation to the ovaries that stay in place and they go into "shock" temporarily. Generally, I find that these symptoms improve over time as the ovaries adapt to the new situation.

When women have an orgasm, the uterus contracts 12 -15 times. This is generally perceived as pleasurable. However, as women age, we see that those same contractions can be uncomfortable. So, in other words, sometimes a hysterectomy improves sexual functioning, sometimes it does the opposite. Most women report to me that sex is better as they age. This is a statement that I will mention time and time again in this book. Yes, there are things that improve with maturity!

Another reason why sex may be better after hysterectomy deals with the reason why so many uteri are removed. A large number of the 620,000+ yearly hysterectomies done in this country are because of abnormal uterine bleeding. As many couples stop having intercourse while the woman is on her cycle, it stands to reason that after hysterectomy, women can have sex at any time instead of waiting for the periods to stop. Therefore, better sex.

There are less fears of pregnancy after a hysterectomy as well so sexual satisfaction may be improved for those who get pregnant "just by thinking about it".

Not every woman however describes better sexual functioning after hysterectomy. Here are some of the common reasons: There is typically a waiting period after surgery that is required. As I mentioned previously, once sex stops for a while, it is difficult to reinitiate. Another reason deals with the symbolism of the uterus. Removing it can be associated with the feeling of being less feminine; less of a woman. Even though it is not visible, removing a uterus can be very emotional to some women. After all, this organ is really what defines some women. It was the "home" of their babies and without it they are no longer able to reproduce. Depression can even be seen on occasion. In my practice, this is rare but certainly I hear about it and can empathize with the ladies. We also have some couples who are afraid of having sex after hysterectomy that was done for cancer reasons, because one or both of them are afraid of transmitting cancer. People who worry about this will be reassured that this is almost never the case.

As I mentioned before, when both ovaries are removed surgically there is a significant change in circulating hormone levels. During residency, I was trained to believe that once a woman reaches 50 years old, the ovaries became inactive and were only there to catch cancer. We were encouraged to remove them if we did surgery in that area. However, more recently we are recognizing that leaving the ovaries even on a 60, 70 or 80 year old woman actually improves life expectancy. I have seen over and over again in women under 50 that when the ovaries are removed there is a significant loss of libido, which I believe is hormonal.

That being said, many women ask me to remove the ovaries when I am "in there" doing surgery. Their main reason usually includes the fear of cancer. Someone in their family or they know had ovary cancer and they know that it is a very difficult to diagnose early. Symptoms are vague like feeling full or some pelvic swelling and tests are unreliable or expensive. It is miserable disease to die from. Also, a long history of pain or cysts and the concern that sometimes the ovaries scar down to the upper part of the vagina causing sexual pain cause them to request oophorectomy (ovary removal).

At the time of hysterectomy, sometimes an extra amount of vaginal tissue is removed, which can shorten the vagina. This is a standard technique when dealing with certain female cancers. This may lead to pain. Fortunately, with persistence, the vagina will usually elongate enough to allow for normal intercourse.

3.17 At what age do women stop having climaxes?

Mrs. H is a very pleasant 74 year old married woman. She still has her uterus and remains sexually active. Yes, she still has pleasurable orgasms, there is no pain associated with them. I think that she asked me that question because she was worried that they would go away. She seemed relieved when I reassured her that there really is no age at which orgasms just go away.

4
Sexual Pain Disorders

4.1 Even using lube and being really gentle, sex still hurts. What can I do?

Question 3.3 got into this issue in some detail. Now, let's look deeper into the cause of the pain. We mentioned introital, deep and post-coital dyspareunia (sex pain). There are some very real reasons for sexual pain in women. We call this "organic" reasons as compared to psychological reasons. After we exclude lubrication issues, we often find generalized estrogen loss. This thins the vaginal tissues making intercourse more likely to hurt. Obviously, estrogen replacement may help. However this is not for everyone. If you opt for estrogen therapy, it is imperative to discuss the various options with your provider. Some questions that you might want to bring up include: Where does this estrogen come from (from soy, yams, horse urine, clover…)? What route should I take estrogens (by skin cream, oral, sublingual, patch, vaginal cream, vaginal pill, injection…)? How long should I take this estrogen (months or years)? What type of estrogen do you recommend (Estrone, Estradiol, Etriol, etc.)? What side effects can I expect (breast tenderness, bleeding, bloating, etc.)?

It should be noted that estrogen replacement is not for everyone. There are some groups of women who shouldn't get any estrogen. If you are prone to getting blood clots, then you should not use estrogens. Most authorities also agree that if you have had breast cancer recently, you shouldn't take estrogens either.

You may chose also not to take them for other reasons.

Introital dyspareunia is fairly common. In fact, just today I saw a lady who healed poorly after her last child. She has a band of tissue that crossed in front of the vaginal opening. It is obvious that every time they try to make love, that tissue gets in the way and hurts her. I recommended a simple in-office procedure that would remove that band and make it more likely for them to have successful intercourse. Scarring can also occur from radiation damage and surgery. We will also see women come in with complaints of vaginal pain involving intercourse and find tears. A few years ago, I met a woman of about 65 years of age. She had be sexually inactive for perhaps 10 or 15 years and found a younger, male partner. After doing some drinking, they started to have intercourse only to find a very large amount of vaginal bleeding occurring. When I saw her in the Emergency Department, there was a deep vaginal tear that required stitches. More typically, sex happens before the vagina has time to stretch and lubricate, which leads to tears. This can occur with the patient's regular partner or a new partner. If they take their time, even if there is a large size discordance (that is a euphemism for small vagina, big penis), often things will be comfortable for both parties. Interestingly, arteriosclerosis (hardening of the arteries) can decrease vaginal blood flow leading to less lubrication.

A word about lubricants. Most of my patients who need personal lubricants use Astroglide, KY gel or Replens. There are so many products now, that it is hard to figure out which to use. Should you use the warming type, the gel, inserts, flavored, etc.? Some people get sensitivity reactions from the ingredients and in others, the glycerin (glycerol, glycerine) can be converted to sugars which is associated with yeast infections. When I counsel women about lubricants, we try to figure out what kind of needs she has. Some women are very embarrassed and tell me that they feel "old" when they end up needing lubrication. Replens is a better option for these ladies since it last a few days, they don't need their partner to know about it and there is no interruption in love making. Others care more about costs so cheaper is better. Also remember that some oil based lubricants can weaken latex condoms, but they tend to work better in water (hot tubs, pools, the ocean) since they will not wash out. A word about taste: if glycerin or a variant is listed in the ingredients, chances are that it will taste sweet.

    Deep dyspareunia involves pain with thrusting; therefore it is sometimes also called thrust dyspareunia. Usually I hear about this type of pain when sex is hurried. The woman's vagina will stretch with sexual excitement making it less likely that her partner will hit something that is uncomfortable. Spend more time on foreplay! Another common reason for this pain is sexual positioning. For example, if a woman has a retroverted uterus meaning it is tilted backwards, then the hand and knees position ("doggy style") will usually hurt more. For these ladies, female superior works better mainly because she can control the depth and angle of penetration. Missionary position may be uncomfortable if a woman's uterus is tilted forward. I recommend that people experiment and try to find the best position for both parties involved. Endometriosis is when endometrial tissue originating from the lining of the uterus is found outside of the womb. This tissue grows under the influence of female hormones and can cause significant pain; pain with sex, pain with periods, pain with bowel movements, etc. Generally, this pain improves with menopause, but that is certainly not a guarantee. These women may need surgery and medications to control the endometriosis. Cancer likewise can cause pain with sex. This can be directly; when the cancer pulls on tissues and scars the vagina. Or it can be indirectly; commonly this occurs after radiation to the pelvis which causes painful changes to the tissues. Surgery as well can distort normal anatomy. When procedures are performed for vulvar or uterine cancer for example, a lot of extra tissue is sacrificed to minimize the chance of leaving behind cancer cells. In many cancer operations, the vagina can be shortened significantly. This may save the life of the patient but it can be at the expense of future dyspareunia. Removal of ovaries at the time of surgery will reduce the amount of circulating female hormones. This may lead to vaginal dryness and poor tissue elasticity and strength. Even though menopause will gradually reduce hormone levels, surgical removal of the ovaries (oophorectomy) does this overnight.

4.2 Why do I now have pain with orgasm?

Orgasmic pelvic pain becomes more common as women age. Those uterine contractions which may feel good in youth can be painful with increasing maturity. That is why sometimes removing the uterus (for other reasons than dysorgasmia obviously) can lead to better sexual functioning in many women. The female orgasm involves the rhythmic contraction of the uterus which may also pull on other organs. Internal scar tissue (adhesions) can bind the uterus to sensitive structures. Many times in surgery, I find adhesions that are attaching the pelvic organs to other sites. For example, commonly the uterus is scarred to the abdominal wall, the ovaries to the intestines and the tubes to the uterus. When the uterus moves, it may pull other structures causing pain. After I remove the scar tissue, many women feel better. The scar tissue itself can cause pain with sex alone or also with orgasm.

Many muscles additionally contract with orgasm, some of which may be in spasm also causing pain. Nerves normally pass through muscles and can become entrapped in muscular spasms.

We are also recognizing more and more the reality of orgasmic headaches. These types of migraines can be quite intense and distressing for those who have to deal with them. They can last up to about 24 hours and males typically get these more than females, which is the opposite of most migraine types. Treatment is available once your provider has established that the headaches are benign in nature. Antimigraine medications often can be useful, these include the triptans such as Imitrex, Maxalt, Frova, etc. Sometimes orgasm can cure a migraine, it really depends on the type of headache and the individual person. In one study done at the Headache Clinic at Southern Illinois University, 47.4% had complete relief of their migraines with orgasm.[8]

On the other hand, we commonly hear that sex and orgasm helps with pain. It stands to reason that if you are focused on a pleasurable activity, your other aches and pains may be temporarily less recognized. In addition, the release of endorphins (your natural pain killers) can also help with the pain.

4.3 I know that women can have pain with sex but how common is it for men?

Sexual discomfort is not only seen in women. Males can have pain with erection, intercourse and ejaculation. The penis becomes erect when there is blood that accumulates in the corpora cavernosa. These are essentially spongy tissues that fill up like balloons when vessels let in more blood. As pressure increases, the penis becomes erect.

Various conditions can lead to erection pain like chordee,

Peyronie's disease, phimosis and priapism. Chordee is a condition in which the erect penis is bent, usually downwards by some tethering. Pain can occur because of the abnormal pressure in the penis with erection or also because of difficulty having intercourse. About 50% of males with Peyronie's disease have pain, however it is due to hard plaques that form within the penis. Phimosis occurs in uncircumcised males when the foreskin can not retract over the erect penis causing pain. Think of it like a mini-tourniquet. Genital injury can likewise cause erectile pain. Priapism is the prolongation of an erection that can be painful even without sexual stimulation. If an erection lasts more than four hours I recommend that the male seek medical care. Long term damage can occur if not. Certain medications can cause this including Desyrel, Thorazine and some illegal ones.

Many women use Intrauterine Devices (IUD). These are long term use products that sit inside the uterus to reduce bleeding and for contraception. There are strings that are attached to the IUD that hang out from the cervix into the vagina. These strings help improve contraceptive efficacy, make it easier to remove the IUD as well as being a convenient reminder that the IUD is still in place. Now for my analogy: if you run your fingers through a child's hair who has a crew cut the hair feels prickly. In a child with longer hair, the hairs feel softer. In much the same way, if the IUD strings are short, males may feel them as spiky during intercourse. Because of this, I usually trim the strings long so when someone calls with a complaint from their partner, I know that something has shifted pulling up the strings.

Vaginismus was discussed in question 3.3. If the vaginal muscles or walls are too tight then male sexual pain can also be a problem. The friction can be uncomfortable or sometimes, he can't even get into the vagina. Vaginal dryness can cause pain in males as well.

Women may have pelvic organ prolapse issues such as a cystocele, enterocele, rectocele, etc. These situations involve weakness to the pelvic support structures. Women come in saying "Doc. My bladder is dropping" or "I think that my uterus is falling out," for example. The pelvic organ prolapse does not usually cause pain for either partner, in fact sex can temporarily improve symptoms for many. Rather it is the surgery for these women that can cause scarring of the vagina. This, in turn, can cause sexual pain for both partners. In addition, non-absorbable mesh is being used more commonly for additional support in vaginal repair surgery. We are finding that the mesh can erode through the vaginal skin in about 8% of cases. Patients and their partners may feel this during sex as a scratchy or prickly area.

Sexual migraines are also more common in males (see question 4.2). Post-ejaculatory pain may be seen with prostate inflammation (prostatitis).

Various dermatology diseases can affect the penis as well. A very common problem, particularly in diabetic males, is yeast infections. This is also known as jock itch. Friction during sex can be painful. Sexually transmitted infections (STIs) are classic for causing pain "down there" especially with urination.

Sexual activities can cause non-genital pain in both genders. Angina may be felt with sex. Patients with lung diseases such as emphysema and asthma may have to limit the amount of stimulation as they can get significantly short of breath. Consider taking your medications such as inhalers before sex or have some oxygen available. Some of my patients have told me that their partner weighs too much. Having a few hundred pounds lying on top of you can not be very comfortable. Many seniors have joint mobility issues such as arthritis or limited range of motion. It may be difficult to achieve certain positions because of this. Specifically with our arthritis patients we find that a warm environment, perhaps after a bath, may be more comfortable for them. As an aside, remember that sex does not have to be a marathon event. There is nothing wrong about taking it slow, stopping periodically, changing positions, etc. In fact, that may be another advantage of age. Youthful goal-oriented sex may be transformed into a process orientation where the end point is less important than the voyage.

4.4 I have pain after sex, not during. They tell me that it is my bladder. Dr. Laury, what am I supposed to do about that?

It sounds like you may be getting recurrent bouts of bladder inflammation and/or infection. This is so common in women that we gave it a name: "Honeymoon Cystitis". Usually, it occurs when there is a change in sexual patterns. For example, when a virginal woman gets married and starts having intercourse. Or, when a woman finds a new partner and she becomes more sexually active. The theory is that since the female urethra is relatively short, intercourse pushes bacteria upward into the bladder. They then start multiplying causing the symptoms of urinary frequency, burning and urgency which we call a UTI. Antibiotics typically help with Urinary Tract Infections. Over time, these tend to get better, perhaps the body gets used to the bacteria, but not always. I have many patients who get recurrent bladder infections so I prescribe medications in a different fashion. After they have had three or more UTIs in a year, instead of having them come in every time to test them, I send them home with extra antibiotics. I might have them treat themselves when they feel like they have one, or have them take a pill right after intercourse. They might also use suppressive therapy where they take one pill every day regardless of symptoms. These techniques allow my patients to enjoy sex without the negatives that they had been used to.

Intercourse can also cause post-coital pain when the vagina is lacking adequate estrogens because the tissues become more fragile. After sex, there can be a burning or soreness. Estrogens, lubricants, more foreplay – these all will help.

There is a syndrome called Interstitial Cystitis (IC) where there is pain, urinary frequency and urgency that is not related to infection. Typically, these women are treated with antibiotics that temporarily help but do not give long term benefits. By the time someone is officially diagnosed with IC, they have seen about six doctors over six years. We have some good ways of testing for this syndrome that speed up this work up so we can diagnosis it quickly and start therapy. Appendix A has a self-evaluation questionnaire called the PUF questionnaire that we use with Interstitial Cystitis. This screening tool is a very quick and easy test to do that may help your provider consider this diagnosis. It was developed by Dr. Lowell Parsons who I had the pleasure of working with.

Bottom line: if you have post-coital pain, something is not right and I recommend you get in to be evaluated.

4.5 I am so embarrassed to ask this question but I want to know why giving oral sex gets more difficult as I age.

No need to be embarrassed. I can think of a number of reasons why this can be the case. We see more TMJ with age.

People with this problem have problems in the jaw/ skull joint (TemporoMandibular Joint) which can cause pain when opening the jaw. Oral sex can be difficult or impossible because of this. See a dental specialist or physical therapist with expertise for this. Also, people generally need more genital stimulation with age which translates to more time "down there" which would account for your situation. Cramps can occur in any muscle group and may be associated with certain medications. Seniors may sleep poorly and the fatigue makes the sexual exercise more demanding. "Tongue tire" is not that uncommon either. Many older folks have trouble extending their heads backwards so depending on your technique this can cause pain. You might want to try to be creative with a combination of oral/manual stimulation and vibrators. At the receiving end, change positions – we know that seeing your partner naked, up close and personal is stimulating for most people so use that information to your advantage. Position yourself so they can get additional stimulation by seeing you work your magic; turn up the lights, use mirrors, place yourself over them… Ask for feedback to achieve a quicker orgasm if that is the problem.

    See, asking that question wasn't too bad. Probably many other people had the exact same question and now they can learn from your input. Thank you for asking.

5
Partner Issues

5.1 My husband is a terrible lover. What can I do?

Poor lovemaking skills are common. After all, there is no high school or college level course that I know of in sexual technique. Most of what is done is modeled on experience and the media. There is a tremendous amount of information out there which may be confusing, dangerous, misinforming or just plain wrong. Most people can be trained though. I find that an open discussion often helps to reassure people that they are normal. Like any skill, it takes practice to improve. What works for one couple might not for another. Communication by far is the most important component here. Over the years working with couples, I found that non-verbal communication can often be more beneficial than spoken instructions. For example, language can be a two edged sword. If a woman tells her husband that he is hurting her or that she prefers another technique, he may become defensive or even just stop making love with her. However, if she guides his hand to show him what she wants, this clearly helps him become a better lover and does it in a non-threatening way. Speaking of communication difficulties, I might suggest the following technique to help change some behavior. One of my patients told me that when they went to parties and her husband got drunk, he would grab her breasts and make sexual comments about her in public which was very embarrassing to her and the other guests. From past experience, she knew that he wouldn't modify his behavior if she just told him to stop it. This would lead to a yelling match. Nothing would change and he would do the same thing at the next party. She tried not going to parties with him. She tried to help him curb his drinking but ultimately, things were still the same. After discussing this with me, we tried a different tactic. I taught her the "I" and "You" substitute word technique where she would explain to her husband how the behavior was affecting her. Previously, she would have said "You are rude and inconsiderate", "You are a nasty drunk" and "You have to change your attitude". Now, she described how the behavior made "me" feel, how "I was embarrassed to go to parties", that "I wanted to be supportive but I was insecure in those drinking situations". This reversed his defensiveness; before he would have felt threatened and lashed out. In the past there was no real incentive to change. However now he was put in a position of wanting to help his wife go out with him. By improving his behavior, he was helping her. This "I" and "You" switch works wonders. Try it!

5.2 Why are there so few eligible partners?

This is a constant complaint from my female patients. I have heard this from 20 year olds on up. Sometimes it is simply an excuse used as protection. You can't get rejected if you don't approach someone; it is safer Other times, it may that the expectations or standards are set too high. I see this particularly often when a widow thinks about romance some time after her partner's death. Her late husband may have been idealized to the point that no one will ever be able to fill his shoes or more accurately, his bed. I think that it is great that she may remember all of the good and forget about his not so good side. And I am not recommending accepting just any romantic overtures; I am however suggesting a realistic appraisal of the situation. Consider that after the age of 85, there will be about 2.6 females around for every 1 male. Even starting at the age of 65, there are still 1.5 females to every 1 male. That is very different than in the younger population. There are slightly more boys born than girls however we males die off earlier than the ladies. In addition, many women marry an older man. The husband is likely to die sooner just because of his decreased life expectancy and because he is older to start with than his wife. Statistically, 48% of women over 60 are widowed as compared to 15% of men. When you look at women and men over 75 the percentages go to 73% and 30% respectively. This lack of partner may explain why only 19% of widows and widowers are sexually active. Compare that to 59% of married men and women.[4]

Men in general are also more sexually active than women. In the NCOA study of 60 year olds, they found that 73% of males had a sexual partner in the last year compared to 56% of women. In older adults, the numbers are 50% of men and 26% of women in their 70s and 80s.[4]

So, what options are available? One is to stick to your guns and not accept anything less than ideal. There is nothing wrong with this but selection will be limited. Another option is to consider a younger partner. Recently, we had a delightful 83 year old woman come in who found a man 20 years younger than she! Go girl! And she had to teach him a few tricks. Though there is not much information on this subject, there seems to be some "sharing" of eligible bachelors, particularly in nursing homes.

Lesbian women have an advantage as they age. There are plenty more women available in terms of actual numbers however they may not be interested in a female partner. Lesbians tend to have more medical problems as well. Some reasons include distrust of the medical community and therefore, they don't keep up with their health maintenance. There is, unfortunately, good evidence that their perceived lack of empathy is grounded in reality. This homophobia is something that needs to change.

5.3 OK, so how do I find new partners?

Finding eligible partners is the same at any age. People need to go out and look. It's like the old story about a guy who complained that he never won the lottery so he stopped playing years ago and he is still not winning! It is highly unlikely that that Mr. or Ms. Right will suddenly show up at your doorstep, unannounced, and both of you proceed to sail into the sunset. You must make yourself found.

Various studies have looked at how people meet. The highest percentage were introduced by friends. This makes a lot of sense as the mutual friends know both parties and have considered compatibility issues. The matchmaker's reputation is also on the line, so they have that as an incentive. Work, church or other religious organizations, ads and health clubs all have brought people together. I often encourage women to go places where like-minded individuals are likely to congregate. If, for example, your passion is music, then go to jazz lectures or classical concerts. Volunteer as an usher at a recital. It is much more likely that you will meet someone with the same interests. If you like nature, go on guided walks or attend the local chapter of native plants society.

While the internet has revolutionized many things, there are some warnings as well. From a positive perspective, some dating sites are doing background checks on applicants so you are less likely to get into a misleading or dangerous situation. Other sites may not be so careful and may allow a lot of misinformation to be listed. The attractive 55 year old professional may actually be much older, less attractive and be out of a job. Photos may have been taken years prior and the information may be out of date. Finally, if you are required to use a credit card, recurrent charges are sometimes hard to stop. I have heard of a few successful alliances over the years but certainly, they are the minority. The other advantage to online dating is that it is relatively cheap compared to paying for a real date that is a bust. Almost predictably, there is even a website that protects women from misleading men (dontdatehimgirl.com). Caveat emptor!

There are travel trips that cater specifically to seniors. Some have an educational component and some are more social in nature. Cruises are a very popular venue for meeting other seniors. There are some companies that are sensitive to your needs (for example, helping you find a roommate if you don't want to spend extra money for a private room). Activities are timed more appropriately for seniors; a good example is that the dances may end by midnight rather than early the next morning. There are other companies that set up sightseeing trips for seniors such as an east coast bus ride along the New Jersey palisades to look at the autumn colors. You can actually go back to school and take college courses geared for seniors. There are reunions of various types. Dances can be a great place to meet folks.

5.4 I am no longer sexually attracted to my husband. What should I do?

I should answer this question with another question. What is it that makes you uninterested in him sexually? This answer will often help me understand the situation better. Referring back to question 5.1, I will expand a bit on this problem. In my practice, there are commonly five reasons why this issue comes up.

Fatigue is very common. We work more days and longer hours than many other countries. Let's say that it is 10 PM when a woman is approached for sex. She may still be attracted to her partner but will decline advances because she would prefer to sleep. This can be interpreted by either partner as a lack of sexual interest or attraction for him though it is neither. The answer here is to make the time for sex. Sex is important; fit it into your schedule.

Depression is also likely. One of the hallmarks of depression is the lack on interest in many activities that are normally enjoyable (anhedonism). I describe it to patients with the following story. "Think about depression as someone who is drowning in the ocean. They are just trying to keep their head above the waves. Sex is just not important enough if you are just trying to stay afloat." Treating the depression will often fix the problem. Unfortunately, some of the therapies can interfere with sexual functioning. In psychotherapy, there is a lot of history and emotions brought back to the surface. This can be emotionally tiring. In addition, people can find that they were attracted to their partner for the "wrong" reason which calls into question the quality of the relationship. My patients often marry their _____. Fill in the blank with "Father", "Mother", etc. Antidepressants can have a negative effect on libido as well. Commonly, many of the popular meds such as Prozac, Paxil, Zoloft … can interfere with the plateau phase (see question 8.3), meaning that it can take longer to achieve an orgasm. This can frustrate folks who eventually give up trying. Males can have orgasmic failure as well. Again, this may seem like a lack of sexual attractiveness to their partner but there are deeper reasons for it.

Sometimes, sexual dysinterest reflects on the entire relationship. Why would someone want to have sex with a rude, self-centered, mean partner? Personal hygiene can also play a role in low libido. Consider how you appear or present to your partner. Can you stand to lose some weight? How about bad breath or body odor? Are you using sex as a reward or withholding sex as a punishment? Is sex an expectation or right rather than requiring permission from a consenting adult?

5.5 How real is ED?

Erectile dysfunction is real. Normally, during sexual arousal, there is an increase in blood flow to the penis through arteries. As the pressure builds up, it compresses the veins that carry blood away. If there is more blood getting in than out, an erection occurs due to the pressure imbalance. ED occurs when this process fails. Though there are many causes for ED, it is clear that the frequency increases with age. From a low of about 10% in men's youth, it can go to a high of about 50% in males over 40 years old. Dr. Irwin Goldstein designed a erection hardness scale that is useful to describe ED. It goes from a 0 (no erection), 1 (larger penis but not hard), 2 (not hard enough for penetration), 3 (hard enough for penetration) to 4 (completely hard and rigid). ED may be associated with poor self-image, depression, anxiety, stress and relationship issues. Sometimes it is actually the other partner who suffers more because they somehow feel responsible for the erection difficulties.

It is important to remember that males, like females, can have certain similar sexual dysfunctions. They can be primary or secondary. Primary meaning that they have always had this issue and secondary describes prior normal functioning with problems at this point in time. Males can also have sexual difficulties because of diabetes, tobacco and alcohol overuse, for example. Other diseases can also be implicated such as certain cancers, heart problems, spinal cord damage and diabetes. Up to 90% of men who are severely depressed have impotence. Low testosterone can impact sexual functioning. Since testosterone levels tend to be higher in the mornings, some men may want to attempt sex at that time to take advantage of that peak. Medications can affect the sexual cycle, particularly the antihypertension and antidepressant drugs. Likewise, smoking actually consticts penile arteries, thereby reducing blood flow. Pelvic surgery is well known to impact on erection quality. Up to 88% of men undergoing abdominal prostate cancer surgery self-report impotence after the surgery.

So, what can be done for these men (besides quitting smoking and starting to exercise)?

Medications called phosphodiesterase type 5 inhibitors can help. Cialis, Levitra and Viagra are examples of these types of drugs. Prostaglandins can act as vasodilators, allowing an increase in blood flow to the penis. Phentolamine probably works on the nerves in the pelvis allowing an erection. Apomorphine (Uprima) is another ED product. Prostaglandin suppositories such as a synthetic E1 type can be placed in the urethra as a suppository (alprostadil [13use]) or injected (Caverject, Edex).

Another product, papaverine, can also be injected directly into the penis to bring on an erection that lasts up to three hours. By relaxing the blood vessel walls, more blood accumulates in the penis, causing the erection. Though multiple daily injections are not generally recommended, there is some literature that shows that a second injection may prolong an erection. Side effects are uncommon. Priapism which is the abnormal maintenance of an erection beyond four hours is a serious but rare complication. Surgery may be necessary to reduce the pressure within the penis that could otherwise cause permanent damage. The injections can also produce penile scarring in up to 15% of users.

  Vacuum pumps (hand pump or battery powered) are devices that fit around the flaccid penis. When activated, the air is removed from the chamber and there is a decrease in pressure within the penis. Blood fills the organ (engorgement). Then, a ring is slipped down to the base of the penis preventing the blood from returning to the body. These devices cost around $400 and may be covered by insurance. Side effects include an abnormal looking penis that can be purplish and swollen. In addition, the ring can interfere with ejaculation; where the semen is not allowed to escape. This should not be dangerous or painful. Up to 80% of users were satisfied with the use of vacuum devices.

  Surgery is also an option. There are mechanical devices and inflatable ones. In one type of surgery, a prosthesis is implanted into the penis. When the man wants to have sex, he straightens out the device giving him an artificial erection. Only about 5 – 10% of ED surgeries are in this category. The majority involve placement of a dual or triple pump system. To achieve an erection, a reservoir implanted in the scrotum is pumped up to distribute fluid into an inflatable device inserted into the penis. After sex, he activates the valve and the erection dwindles. At least 96% of men are satisfied with this technology but it can run up to $23,000, though it may be covered by some insurances. Some people note that the device shortens the length of their penis in relation to what they had previously. Newer techniques have been developed to reduce this problem. In addition, the surgery seems to reduce the likelihood of a natural erection even if the device is removed.

In terms of diagnosis, the nocturnal penile tumescence test is considered the gold standard. By monitoring the variations of erections during the night, this test differentiates between organic or psychological causes of ED. If the problem is psychogenic, then therapy may be of value. If the problem is organic, the above options may be helpful.

5.6 On a similar note, do those vacuum devices that my husband reads about work?

The theory behind these units is that the negative pressure generated by the pump draws in more blood to the penis, thereby giving the user an erection. Yes they work however it involves some getting used to. The temperature of the erect penis tends to be cooler than normal and there can be some purplish discoloration. Incidentally, women now have a similar vacuum unit called the Eros system (see question 2.17 for more details). Other products that you may read about include penile blood flow outflow blockers (rings) and aphrodisiacs (sexual stimulants).

Aphrodisiacs have been around for hundreds if not thousands of years. Just about everything has been tried and/or touted as a cure for impotence. Some of the more exotic ones are described in question 8.6. Yohimbine, on the other hand, obtained from an African shrub, has been shown to improve erectile success. Even though it is mainly studied on men, I have recommended it for my female patients who want to try something (anything!) for their low libido. Usually a 5.4 milligrams dose seems to help a good number of my patients.

Penis rings and holding the penis downwards (towards the feet) make sense from a blood vessel perspective. Erections occur when blood accumulates in the fluid reservoirs inside the penis. The fluid hydrostatically keeps the organ firm. When the blood is allowed to return into circulation, the penis loses its tone. When the blood is blocked from re-entering the blood stream, the man maintains the erection longer. Priapism is the abnormal prolongation of an erection, sometimes lasting for many days. Though it sounds at first blush like a good thing, actually it can be quite painful, can cause permanent damage and may require surgery to treat. So watch what you wish for!

5.7 Dr. Laury, this might sound like a stupid question but do males need an orgasm?

Good question. Simple answer is no. You hear about the need for food, water and shelter. Some experts add Sex to that list however I tend to disagree. People die rapidly without water and somewhat slower without food however I have never heard of anyone passing away because of a lack of sex. I will go out on a limb and say that there has never been a death certificate filled out with the cause of death listing "Lack of Sex". Having said that, I will agree that sexual activity is an important part of being a human. The drive to interact sexually with others affects our entire civilization. Books have been written about sex (including this one); advertisements and movies tap into this need. Entire lives have been affected by the aftermath of sexual deviances such as incest and rape. There are no medical side effects from a lack of ejaculation. So, no, males (and females) don't need orgasms; however, the drive to achieve sexual satisfaction is potentially very powerful.

5.8 My partner ejaculates too soon. What can he do about that?

Unlike women, once men orgasm, there is a refractory period in which no amount of stimulation will result in another climax. Premature ejaculation (PE) can be very frustrating for both partners as the male ejaculated too soon to please his partner. PE is the most common sexual dysfunction in males less than 40 years old. Indeed, it can occur in up to 30% of males and is more common in the younger population. Hurrah for age! There are many theories as to why this occurs. You may hear of the idea that teenagers learn to orgasm quickly because of the fear of getting caught masturbating. Another theory, which has some physiological support, holds that some males have an increased sensitivity on the glans penis. Generally, experts feel that PE is a psychological problem. Though PE can be very emotionally distressing, modern therapies show that about an 85% success rate. So, back to your question. What is available? Anesthetics (sprays, gels, etc.) that numb the penis can be helpful. The downside is that it will numb the man's pleasurable sensations as well as potentially his partner's. Basically, what is the point then? If you use this technique, my recommendation is to use a condom. There are also techniques involving starting to have intercourse then stopping before it is "too late" as well as mental gymnastics to train him to think about something else. The pinch or squeeze and pause therapy is time tested and works. Before a male reaches the orgasmic inevitability, the penis is squeezed forcefully but not painfully until he is able to resume intercourse. One treatment round requires 10 repetitions. Sometimes medications work; the side effects of certain medications, particularly the SSRI antidepressants, include prolongation of the sexual plateau (see question 2.4). If your partner has PE and is able to have an erection fairly soon after ejaculation, allowing him to have an orgasm first can prolong his erection the second time around. However, remember that the older a man gets, the longer he has to wait until he is able to have another one.

5.9 Questions about wheelchair bound individuals, obese folks, amputees, people with dentures…

I hear these questions commonly and perhaps surprisingly, the answer is rather similar. Be Creative! Often what seems like a negative can be converted to a more positive experience. As an example, people sometimes complain about using condoms, how it spoils the spontaneity…. Yet, everyone knows that they can reduce the chance of getting some sexually transmitted infections (STIs). Having a partner help the male put a condom on as part of the foreplay can be fun and sensual. It also signals that intercourse will be happening fairly soon and it demonstrates that you care about hygiene and protection which goes both ways. The same applies to taking off a prosthetic leg or removing your dentures. Consider it foreplay!

Don't assume that someone else will be turned off sexually by some of your perceived negativism. There are folks who are stimulated by amputees, who like urine play (so incontinence may be a plus) or who prefer oral sex with an edentulous person who can not hurt them because they don't have teeth to do so. Additionally, even if you have a medical problem, they may also have the same situation. In fact, you may have met because you share similar situations. When a couple comes into the office and we talk about sexual hang-ups, it is gratifying to hear that most of the time what the first partner considers a big turn off is hardly noticed by the other partner. The two most common issues that I hear about include leaking some urine with orgasm and being overweight. Almost invariably, the second partner is not bothered by it to the same extent.

Other issues to work through include limited mobility or the wheelchair bound partner. I would encourage folks to be open to creativity and to use good communication. As it turns out, some paraplegic and quadriplegic patients get sexual sensations through non-sexual stimulation. If they can't feel their genitals, they may still feel a caress on their arm or back. Orgasms may still occur with or without genital stimulation. Though some folks may not feel the orgasm directly, there is still the "feel good" neurochemical cascade that they will appreciate. Having a partner help the wheel chair person sexually can also be very satisfying. Remember that aside from actually having sex, watching your partner undress or stimulate themselves ranks very highly as well. Solutions are sometimes simple. For example, my rheumatoid arthritis patients usually feel increasing painful by the evening so they can consider sexual activity earlier in the day. If they have trouble using a vibrator because they can't grip it easily, I recommend putting it in a foam ball that can be obtained at any sports store. My osteoarthritis and fibromyalgia folks may find that sex in the hot tub works better for them. For some patients with major pain, say cancer or recovering after a surgery, watching their partner masturbate can be an adequate substitute.

In a large study by the NCOA, at least 50% of respondents stated that it was important for their partner to be able to take part in and enjoy sex. When asked specifically on how important sex was to the relationship more men than women felt that it was "very" or "somewhat" important. However even there, about 50% of women felt that way.[4]

5.10 How do medical conditions in general affect sexual satisfaction and activity?

The NCOA study actually looked into that as well. They found that when partners were available, 51% of men and 12% of women did not have sex because of their medical condition. In 13% of men and 44% of women, they didn't have sex because of a medical condition in their partner. Some medical conditions also required medications that can affect sex. All of these impacted on their sexual contentment.[4]

5.11 I want to make a good impression. What are other people looking for in me?

The NCOA asked seniors what they looked for in a sexual partner. Ninety percent said that a high moral character, a pleasant personality, a good sense of humor and intelligence were important qualities. Other less important issues include financial security. You will please note that physical beauty was not on that list. More women than men were likely to seek financial security in a partner (85% of women vs. 56% of men) and seek a partner who observes a religious faith (72% of women vs. 58% of men). Men were more likely to seek a partner who is interested in sex (76% of men vs. 46% of women) and who has an attractive body (67% of men vs. 48% of women).[4]

5.12 My husband says that he can't have an erection but some mornings that is not the case. Is he lying to me?

Nocturnal Penile Tumescence (NPT) is a normal state in males from toddler on where there is a spontaneous erection during sleep. Teenagers generally have up to 90 minutes of erection per night which slowly decreases to about 20 minutes in a seventy year old man. NPT is associated with Rapid Eye Movement (REM) sleep most of the time.[6] There are various testing protocols to document if a man has nocturnal erections which help differentiate between ED of a psychological or organic reason. In your husband's case, it is likely psychological issues since he clearly can have erections. Only about 10 percent of ED is psychological but it may response well to therapy. Please read question 5.5 for more options.

Here is an interesting story about testing for NPT. Testing equipment is available but can be quite expensive and is not always accessible. Apparently some enterprising folks in Africa needed to test men but couldn't afford the instrumentation. Their solution was to stick a line of stamps around the base of the penis in the evening. If, in the morning, the perforations were broken then erectile function was assumed. I would guess that they used one cent stamps or equivalent to save costs! I don't know if this is a true or anecdotal but it makes for a good story.

6
Social and Privacy Issues

6.1 I am a 74 year old woman who is living with my daughter and her husband. Even though I would like to have a gentleman over, I don't see how that could work out. What suggestions do you have?

You bring up some very important points. Many fixed income seniors live with their family. Sometimes, seniors live with their family for companionship or because of health concerns. Like many things in life, this has advantages and disadvantages. Financially, living with your daughter may be more affordable. There is the possibility of camaraderie. Certainly, it may be safer for you if you fall or have a stroke for example. For the many folks who no longer drive, there is some extra help available for appointments and events. Living with family can be beneficial to them as well. Often, you can act as a live-in babysitter or just watch the house while they are away. With so many people needing financial help these days, your input is welcomed. A lifetime's experience is there for you to share as well.

The down side must also be considered. As you mentioned, there is the potential loss of privacy. In your own home, you can dress any way that you please, make as much noise as you want and entertain without restriction. Sharing a home can limit that independence. Inviting someone over can cause tension; for you, your guest and your family. Our society tends to devalue sexuality as we age. Seniors are portrayed as asexual (see question 2.10). One unspoken fear that might be playing a role in your situation deals with inheritance. Consciously or not, they realize that if you remarry, there may be less of an estate to go around after your death. Therefore, your guest may be considered a threat to their future finances. This is the ugly truth in some situations. One option that may settle things down a bit involves setting up trusts and funds that would go to your children regardless of if you remarry. A prenuptial agreement with your future husband will also be seen as less threatening.

Children in general are stressful. They definitely have their benefits but most families welcome the eventual "empty nest" when it finally happens. It may seem like today we see adult children stay at home longer. One thought is that there is a work ethic problem in our youth. Another theory is that things cost more so our kids don't have enough to put as a down payment for their own house.

Another hidden secret is elder abuse. This involves exploitation, injury or mistreatment by someone they depend on for care or protection. By one estimate[9], this occurs in 2 to 10% of the time. Looking at this from another angle, the National Research Council Panel to Review Risk and Prevalence of Elder Abuse and Neglect estimates that one to two million seniors are abused. In addition, around 92% of these abuses are never brought to the attention of the authorities. Abuse can have many different faces. The most common is neglect. Care is limited which may include feeding, medication administration, environmental temperature control, etc. There is also physical, emotional, financial and, the least common, sexual abuse. Most often the perpetrator is an adult child, usually a son. For more information and education, the National Center on Elder Abuse has excellent resources. In a housing situation where the senior is isolated from other people, this abuse may not be recognized by others. I consider this situation when I see older women with excessive bruises or even fractures that defy a good explanation. The most suspicious sign in my office is when the "caretaker" never gives her any privacy with me and answers all of the questions for her. Reporting of these crimes generally comes from a health care provider followed by a family member in order of frequency. The shocking part is that only 3.8% of victims self-report their abuse.

6.2 I recently went over a widow's house. The place was so loaded with her late husband's presence that I felt guilty even thinking sexually about the lady. I would like for this relationship to progress but what should I do about it?

One of the realities of getting older is that you will bury your friends and family. Death is part of life. Though, most older folks don't fear death for themselves, they mourn those who passed on before they do. It is understandable that after 10, 30 or 60 years together there will be a normal grieving process. For some seniors, they will never have another partner. However, for others, they may not be willing to give up that component of their life. Helping people through a loss is difficult but I feel that it is critical from a physician's perspective. Over the year's I have had to counsel families who have loss pets, children, spouses and parents. Acting on this responsibility takes time and empathy. Typically, there is a time of depression and adjustment after a partner's death. This can easily last six months or more. Incidentally, there is some emerging information on the benefits of short term use of a benzodiazepine (Valium, Xanax, Ativan…) to improve sleep and decrease pathological grieving. It is not meant to make the memories go away or shorten the process. It is meant to reduce the obsessions that often accompany a significant loss, the endless loop of thoughts that actually burn into the brain the hurt.

When the time comes to resume social activities, it is important to understand that your late partner would likely not want you to dedicate the rest of your life to their memory at the expense of your well being. Think of it from the opposite perspective. Let's say you die first and leave your spouse behind. Looking down on the situation from you new otherworld vantage, would you really want them to stay in mourning the rest of their life and give up the possibility of finding happiness again in the future? Once someone understands this, the next step is to help the process along by becoming more sociable. Start by going out with friends in a group. Try going to some social or religious activities. Go to a health club or a music recital. One of the best option is to get a pet. Dogs need daily exercise, they help you interact with others and they are always happy to see you.

Perhaps a bit later, consider go to events as a double date. Sometimes afterward, you may want to start dating one on one. When that time approaches, think about things from this new person's viewpoint. How would he/she feel if they enter your shrine, so to speak, devoted to your dead spouse? Could you perhaps consolidate memorabilia so it is not obvious everywhere? Think hard about removing their "presence" in the bedroom. It is a big turn off to have a late partner looking over your shoulder while making love for the both of you. When you do this environmental review you may also want to minimize the kids' and grandkids' photos as well.

6.3 A very weird thing happened to me the other day and I wanted to share the experience with you. I treated myself to a massage and I started crying uncontrollably.

I have many massage therapists as well as physical therapists as patients in my practice. Speaking with them, they have all had the same experience among their clients. Since your emotional response seems universal, I would venture to say that you were responding to the human touch rather than the muscle pain. Getting older doesn't take away your feelings and needs. You may not have been touched compassionately by a fellow human in some time and touch can bring back many memories for some. Remember too that there are different types of touch. Most non-sexual touch in our society is prefunctory; think of a handshake. Interestingly, sexual touch can also be superficial. Some feel that kissing is more erotic than intercourse. It may be that it is easier to "go elsewhere" when the partner is not face to face. Authentic non-sexual touch is rare and may remind you of childhood, hence the emotional link.

6.4 I started dating again and found a man who I thought was right for me. We had sex and now I really feel bad about doing it with him. Am I abnormal?

Sexual regret is common. Oswalt and others did a study where they found that 72% of people regretted, at least once, their decision to have sex. The most common reasons mentioned included going against their morals, doing it under the influence of alcohol and realizing that what they wanted out of it was different than their partner's[10]. This is good information for us to share with folks as it may help them work through their experience.

7
Psychological Issues

7.1 After a long battle with prostate cancer, Lothar was laid to rest. I have not had relations for over 10 years. Dr. Laury, I think that I am ready to resume but how?

Studies show that the longer the wait, the less likely it is for people to resume sex. In my practice, I find that this is generally true within an intact marriage. I have plenty of patients who have not had intercourse with their spouse for 10 or more years even though they live in the same household. The most common reasons that I hear about include ED (see question 5.5), alcoholism and dysfunctional marriages. After a while, many people just give up trying. On the other hand, there are plenty of folks who resume sex successfully after their partner's death. They learn to get on with their life. The biggest complaint that I hear is the lack of available partners (see question 5.2). Sometimes I need to get someone to see that they may never find a soul mate who exactly replaces their deceased partner. They have to decide if their level of expectation may be set too high. Obviously, this is treading on very emotional ground. Guilt can also be a heavy burden for some people. There are issues related to loyalty and betrayal that need to be dealt with.

From a medical perspective, I educate ladies about sexually transmitted infections (STIs), vaginal lubricants and we talk about estrogens. If on pelvic exam there is serious thinning and shrinkage of the vaginal tissues, they may want to try vaginal estrogens. There are vaginal pills, creams, rings, etc. I am able to reassure some ladies that intercourse is likely to be successful when I tell them that they just tolerated a speculum or vaginal exam. This information may ease their mind as it shows them that the tissues are flexible enough to make sex successful in the majority of cases.

7.2 My wife doesn't want to have sex with me any more. She says that she is too fat and old for that. Yes she has gained some weight and is a bit older but I still find her attractive. What is going on here?

Without the benefit of meeting with her, my first guess would be that she may be depressed. Among the common symptoms of depression, there is anhedonism. This expresses itself as a lack of interest in things that normally are enjoyable such as sex, eating at restaurants, going out to movies, etc. Weight gain is also seen, particularly in women. Finally, she says things that sound negative or pessimistic. Depression is understood to be due to a complex interaction between genetics and environment. It is more common in women. Besides the toll that it takes on the individual, it also impacts on the family and friends. There is also a high mortality associated with this disease. My strong advisement is to bring her in to see a health care provider where she can get diagnosed and treated.

Since about 60% of folks with depression also have coexisting anxiety, it is important to realize that sexual dysfunction can be due to either or both of these diseases. Anxiety can manifest itself in many forms. Performance anxiety is common. A man may be worried that he will ejaculate too early or a woman may be insecure with her body being exposed. The inability to relax enough to enjoy relations is sometimes part of this as well. I have a number of patients who have been raped in the past which, without a doubt, influences their sexual functioning.

Let's talk more about sexual attractiveness. Beauty is definitely in the eye of the beholder. Among our patients, we have some stunning women who are models, actors, TV personalities, etc. Yet, many of them feel that they are ugly. If they are asked if they are attractive, they invariably will say "No". Part of their problem may be insecurity and depression. In order to help them, I may send them to psychologists or treat them with antidepressants. Another trick that seems to help is to enlist their partner in an office visit. When asked, usually the partner will say that they are sexually attracted to them. This takes the focus off of the other individual. Despite her concerns about sagging breasts or stretch marks, she may learn that her partner finds her attractive just the way she is. Remember not to take things personally; there may be other reasons for her lack of interest.

7.3 Why is it that my husband usually wants sex in the evening, when I am tired?

Fatigue probably represents one of the top three reasons why my patients don't want to have intercourse. When given the choice between sleep and sex, the former generally wins out. So, back to your question. Why is it that males often approach their partners in the evening? It certainly is not their testosterone levels peaking. As we mentioned previously, that occurs in the morning. One possibility is that sex helps many people sleep better. There is some truth to the observation that after sex, many males roll over and go to sleep. You may be their sleep aide! Another reason is probably that you have recently gotten undressed and are going to bed. Remember that in many males, these actions can be a powerful sexual stimulant. According to some psychologists, there is a hierarchy of needs that humans follow. As the most pressing needs are met (such as food, water, shelter…), the next level of needs can be fulfilled. Sex is one of these next levels. In the morning, he has priorities such as getting ready for work, showering, shaving, etc. In the evening, he has met most of these needs and is attempting to fulfill his sexual needs. The truth is that we just don't know. Some men want sex in the morning, some in the evening, some never and some at anytime. I would recommend that you discuss this with him, and make time for relations when both of you are interested.

Excessive fatigue can also cause mood changes and an increase in pain sensitivity. Consider adequate rest as therapy.

7.4 I was brought up in an era where single women just did not pursue men. I am now a widow and I am having a difficult time finding companionship. What can you recommend?

I find that some women cling to archaic ideas about sexuality. We now know much more about sex than 50 years ago. Some of the things that you may have been taught may not be true and there may have been a lot of misinformation. It is unlikely that some man will just show up on your doorstep and ask to be the new part of your life. I applaud you for considering a return to social functioning and for asking your question. To achieve meaningful contacts with others, you need to learn how to initiate the opportunity. There is nothing "wrong" with asking someone to dance or to go to a show or a movie. Old fashioned ideas will likely reduce the possibility of finding someone. Go to festivals and events or volunteer some time at a club, library or hospital. Go up to someone and start a conversation. While many of these things may be outside of your comfort zone, they are important if you want to meet people. Remember the worst thing that can happen is that they say "No". Other women tell me that they feel as if they should act their age. What does that mean? Does that mean that after a certain age, people should abandon sex and the pursuit of happiness? I actually think that with advancing age, our inhibitions decrease. It's like the poem about wearing purple.

I am not suggesting that you forget about your morals. I am however suggesting that you re-evaluate how valid some of those ideals really are. If you don't believe in sex before marriage, you still need to find that significant other to get married to.

Another old fashioned idea was that one simply did not masturbate. Apparently self-stimulation led to mental feebleness, warts, hairy palms and host of other problems. Now, we know better. Not only is it common, it also confers health benefits. In my practice, I feel that sometimes I need to "give permission" to some ladies to masturbate. One poor lady was distraught six months out of the year and then fine again for six. It turns out that her husband was a fisherman in Alaska while she stayed home in Oregon. After I talked to her about solo-sex, she felt much less guilty about what she was already doing. I covered this topic in greater detail in question 2.13.

7.5 It has been so long since I have even considered dating someone. How do I know if we are compatible?

There is no correct answer to this one. What has worked in the past may no longer be the case. What may be acceptable to you may be intolerable to someone else. Patients have told me that they can't be in the same bedroom as their husband because he snores too loudly and yet others have told me that they can't sleep when their husbands are gone because they miss the snoring. Remember that a relationship is a two person dance. Your partner comes into the alliance with their baggage and you have yours. Generally speaking, both of you will need to work at keeping the union functioning. The psychology behind why some people are attracted to certain individuals is also fascinating. There are all sorts of cues that are involved. Some people marry their ideal persona, some their parents, others like "bad boys"… I know of one woman on her ninth marriage. It seems to me that she has more to learn from previous experiences. From the other perspective, there are marriages that are very unhappy and unhealthy for everyone involved and yet they stay together for many reasons. I have heard hundreds of times that they stay together for the "kids' sake". Believe me when I tell you that most kids are not stupid. They observe and understand perhaps more than we might give them credit for. In addition, when kids are grown up, you are not really protecting them by staying together.

I would encourage you to find someone who has at least some similarities in taste, culture and interests. Someone who you are not afraid of. Someone who treats you with respect. Test drive the relationship. Don't worry too much about just being yourself. Honesty goes a long way towards keeping a relationship viable.

7.6 My hubby has heart problems. How do I know if it is OK to have sex with him?

The answer touches on two different issues. One deals with the benefits and risks to him. The other unstated part brings up matters of role change. Depending on who you read, sexual intercourse is the energy equivalent as running up two to nine flights of stairs. Vigorous sex may burn around 200 calories and the heart rate can double. If he can do that without serious health concerns then sex ought to be fine. Some cardiologists are very conservative and advise no sex after certain procedures or events for some specific length of time. Others may be able to quantify the amount of exercise tolerance based on experience and testing. After a myocardial infarction ("MI," "heart attack"), people are often advised to avoid sex for up to 3 months though this is not supported by much evidence.[11] The best answer really comes from his provider.

Despite the popular idea that sex and heart disease are a dangerous combination, nurses have told me that all of the male hospital patients they take care of, cardiac folks tend to act out the most sexually. There is inappropriate comments, looks and contact. It probably reflects concerns of death, self-sufficiency and self-confidence. You can expect similar anxieties at home. Your question also supports the finding that most people are more worried about the cardiac patient's health than the person with the problem himself worries.

Chest pain patients (angina) often find that exercise increases their discomfort so modification of sexual technique may be helpful. Remember though, that if he takes nitrates like nitroglycerin, he can also not use meds like Viagra. Heart failure patients are often limited by the amount of exercise that they tolerate (in this case sex). Exercise, however it is part of their therapy.

Life deals with change. Everyone went from a dependent child to an adult with responsibilities. You may have become a wife or husband, perhaps an equal in your relationship. When one partner becomes ill and needs care, the relationship changes. Privacy issues can change dramatically. Independence can be altered. Think about changing someone's diapers or cleaning surgical wounds compared to going for walks and giving massages. Caretakers do tremendous of amount of work. It is a 24 hour a day, 7 days a week labor. It can easily become overwhelming. I have seen 98 lbs. women trying to help their 200 + lbs. husband out of a wheelchair. Studies show that caretakers tend to have poorer health, develop more cancers, postpone their own care and die sooner than their peers. Financially, they also do worse, often becoming financially destitute as a result. The sense of obligation is immense for some people, to the exclusion of themselves. In terms of your husband, it may be hard to mentally convert from nurse to lover. In addition, it is very common to have fears of killing or at least speeding up cardiac patients' demise by having sex with them. Some people are afraid that they will expire during sex. On the other hand I had patients whose husbands told me that they had no such fears and, by the way, "that would be way to go, doc!"

Role change may also apply to you if you are living with adult children. There can be quite the reversal, from caretaker to care receiver. You and the kids may have a difficult time adapting to the new relationship. For more information, you may want to reread question 6.1.

7.7 My friends are trying to set me up with other men however I really don't have the interest right now. How can I make them understand this?

Sometimes, friends mean well but may be overly enthusiastic about helping. Some questions that you may want to ask yourself are: Why are you not interested in meeting new people? Are you depressed? Are you still grieving for a past partner? Are your friends really pitying you rather than have your best interests in mind? Are your friends absolutely right to try and get you to go out and you are being stubborn?

Once you understand where your disinterest is coming from, it may be easier to respond to your friends. Going out with new men is not the best way of dealing with depression. Getting in to see a health care provider is better. They may suggest therapy or medication. Commonly, I find insomnia is the cause of the depressed feelings not a result of it. Improving a patient's sleep can work wonders on their mood.

Processing grief takes time. Typically, people go through a normal sequence of events after a loss. This can be a loss of a life partner, loss of health, loss of money, etc. The first step usually is Denial where you may not be able to accept the reality of the information ("There must be some mistake.", "He is not really dead."). Anger follows and it can be directed at anyone ("He brought this on himself.", "He left us with all of the debt."). Bargaining may be seen next ("Please God, if you bring him back, I will go to church every Sunday, change my ways, donate money…"). Depression then occurs which may last many months. Finally Acceptance sets in. Understanding this process is very reassuring to people as it lets them know that what they are going through is normal. Knowing where you are on the continuum will also help figure out what is coming next and how close you are to getting through this process.

7.8 Am I too old to change my habits?

That is a great question. It shows that you insightful and are thinking about the future. Yes, as people age they tend to be more restrictive in their habits, attitudes, likes and dislikes. Often however, it may be just that you have found what works for you so there is little incentive to change. Change can also be frightening for many; xenophobia is the medical term for this. Going outside of your comfort zone allows you to experience new situations. For every hobby that you enjoy, there was a time where you were inexperienced and not yet skilled. Through education, training and practice you learned. There is more literature coming out all the time that is showing that the brain responds to stimulation with growth. The other way of looking at it is that through a lack of stimulation the brain loses "strength". When a patient asked me if I thought that you can teach old dogs new tricks, I told her "Yes" without hesitation. Brain stimulation is very important. There are many things that you can do to maintain or improve your mental flexibility. Socializing has an amazing capacity to stimulate the neurons; you need to remember people's names, interact with them and verbalize various bits of information. Playing games helps as does studying a new language or skill. I feel so strongly that this is the case that I make it a point of doing something new at least yearly. I have learned how to fly a helicopter, weld, write books (well, I hope!), graft fruit trees, race motorcycles, grow organic mushrooms commercially and rock climb. I have taken linguistic courses and TV directorship and production. Initially, there is a humbling aspect of learning that eventually translates into self-confidence and enjoyment. The moral of this story is that you need to initiate the first step. Go out and start the process.

Remember also that you come from an era which is quite different than today's. Partners and friends who hark back to those times will tend to have the same perspective so actually it can be very comforting to meet and interact with them. Just as you may be opinionated, they too will be likewise. People tend to gravitate towards others with similar tastes, interests, etiquette, habits and language. Finally, remember that you have the same fears and insecurities as the next person.

7.9 I feel uncomfortable bringing up sexual problems with my doctor. Why is it so easy for your patients to talk to you about these personal matters?

First let me say that I don't know if it is easy for my patients to discuss these intimate details with me. They do, however, end up discuss sensitive things with me. Perhaps it has been enough of a problem for them to "bite the bullet" so to speak and bring things up despite the embarrassment. I would hope that by being non-judgmental and sensitive to my patients' social, ethnic, situational and cultural background, they feel more comfortable with me. Many women have stated that I was the only doctor to actually ask if there was a sexual problem. It is pretty clear that most people will not volunteer such information unless specifically asked. A questionnaire can sometimes be useful. Leaving out a few brochures on dyspareunia (sexual pain) for example may help. Many doctors may themselves be uncomfortable with the subject. Remember that we generally don't get very much training in sexual issues. I remember back in medical school just one afternoon of lectures! Providers can also be too rushed to spend the time to adequately answer questions. I have patients that finally, after years of asking them if they have sexual problems, start to talk to me. Think about if it is something that is embarrassing to you or your provider. I would guess that the majority of the time, it is the former. Many of us are knowledgeable in sexual dysfunction and even if we don't know the answer, we can send patients to the appropriate place. Daily, I find that simple education is all that is needed. That is why I put in Chapter 2; "What is Normal". Just yesterday, I had a 20 some year old lady who didn't know that many women have trouble having an orgasm with intercourse. After talking to her, she went home knowing that she is "normal". Much of the material for this book was brought to my attention through these types of patient talks.

I usually preface my discussions with a statement to the effect that I understand that it can be difficult for many people to discuss sexual issues. Once they know that I care, they usually open up and become quite candid. It is also important for me not to assume things. Many a lesbian will not correct a provider if they assume, incorrectly, that she is sexually active with males. Even married women may not be sexually active with their husbands. Some are active with their boyfriends but not with their husbands. So there are many variations and we have seen most of them so start asking questions.

7.10 My wife has early Alzheimer's disease. We continue to have sex but sometimes I don't think that she is really "there". Am I bothering her? Am I helping her? What should I do?

This question really has to do with ethical issues. For example, is your wife mentally competent to consent to sexual activities? Is it OK to go outside of the relationship if she is not competent to allow sex?

My suggestion is to get a provider to evaluate her competency. At that point you have something to work with. Her provider may also have some suggestions in terms of the benefits and risks of sex to her. From the other perspective, some people with neurological deficits have trouble expressing themselves verbally. Physical contact may help bridge this gap.

7.11 Help! I am growing a moustache. Should I sign up for the circus?

Admittedly, having a moustache on the lady's face is usually not considered attractive. Women spend a tremendous amount of energy trying to get rid of these pesky hairs. They usually grow because of genetics, hormonal imbalances, medications and menopause. I have seen upper lip hair on many female teenagers, particularly in certain ethnic groups and those girls with polycystic ovary syndrome. I see it when there are adrenal and ovary tumors. When women take too much testosterone, excess hair is commonly seem. What I think that you are asking about is the normal aging hair increase in women.

The theory that I subscribe to involves ratios. Women put out estrogen and testosterone. During the premenopausal years, the higher estrogen levels "control" the testosterone. As women age, estrogen levels drop significantly but testosterone levels are not reduced quite as much. This allows the testosterone to act more in the body, hence the hair growth.

We can offer hirsute women laser hair removal, waxing, medications, reassurance, etc.

7.12 My wife is depressed and taking medications for it. How does that cause her lack of interest in sex?

One of the common symptoms with depression is a lack of interest in normally enjoyable activities like sex. Unfortunately, treatment of depression can also cause this. Patients often describe sexual side effects from some of their medications (see question 8.3 for a list). In addition, psychotherapy can be emotionally draining which leaves less psychic energy to dedicate to other activities such as sex.

I am fond of describing depression as being in the middle of the ocean. People are treading water, just trying to keep their heads above the waves. Sex is just not high on their list of priorities at that moment. This can put a person's situation in perspective to their significant other who may not understand.

When I was in medical school, we made liberal use of mnemonics. These memory aids helped us remember all of the new information that we were exposed to. **SIGECAPSS** was used to recall the criteria for depression. We needed five of the following nine to consider depression as a diagnosis: **S**leep problems, **I**nterests down, **G**uilt feelings, low **E**nergy, poor **C**oncentration, **A**petite up or down, **P**sychomotor retardation or agitation, excessive **S**adness and **S**uicidal thoughts. I hope that this mnemonic helps you when someone seems depressed to you and you want to quickly run down that possibility.

8
Medications

8.1 I am on Paxil and have trouble getting an orgasm. Is this common?

Actually, yes! In my clinical experience, about 40% of my female patients report this problem. Typically it starts with prolongation of the plateau phase (see question 2.4). Then, if things continue, many couples don't want to deal with the extra amount of work that it takes to bring her to orgasm so they eventually reduce sexual activities. Men, in particular, can have all sorts of medication induced sexual problems. These may include plateau phase prolongation and failed or retrograde orgasm where the ejaculation either doesn't happen or it goes into the bladder. In one publicized study that was presented at the 2001 American Psychiatric Association annual meeting, Researchers Drs. Anita Clayton and James Pradko found that the SSRIs studied (Paxil, Prozac, Celexa and Zoloft) had a high likelihood of sexual dysfunction. After questioning almost 6300 people, they found up to a 43% sexual dysfunction rate. The chances of sexual dysfunction increased when higher doses were taken, when there was a history of past dysfunction with antidepressants, when there was a lower education or financial level and when other medications were also taken. Notably, they also found that as people got older, were married or smoked cigarettes, the chances of sexual side effects increased. The medication that had the least probability of sex problems was Buproprion (Wellbutrin/Zyban). I certainly have seen this clinically in my practice.

So, what to do? Options include: stop the medication, reduce the dose or add another product that hopefully fixes things. We'll go into more specifics a bit later.

8.2 What meds help sex?

It really depends on what you need help with. I tend to prescribe a lot of topical preparations that help heal or soothe the vaginal tissues. For example, if a woman has recurrent yeast infections, intercourse may be uncomfortable. By treating the infection, sex is likely to improve. Similarly, if the vagina is painful then giving someone a topical anesthetic like xylocaine can allow for sex. A disadvantage to these gels is that it also numbs the rest of the genitals which interferes with the whole point of having sex. Males in contact with the vagina will also get the gel or cream on their parts which will reduce their sensitivity as well. This can actually be a plus if there is a problem with premature ejaculation.

Lichen sclerosis is a progressive, intensely itchy skin disease that can affect older women. The vaginal tissues agglutinate (seal together) to the point that intercourse may be impossible without treatment. Sometimes I use steroids and sometimes estrogens. Estrogens are powerful hormones that can often improve sexual functioning by increasing vaginal lubrication and elasticity. The female genital tract has many estrogen receptors. It also can increase clitoral sensitivity and size. In the brain, it may act as a stimulant as well. With all the confusion over estrogens and side effects, I usually have to spend extra time with my patients to see if they are comfortable taking the hormone. Another hormone which is often helpful is testosterone. Also called the "male hormone", it can improve both genders' feeling of well being and sexual interest. In males, it is critical for sexual functioning. Remember that sexual activity in men is 95% hormonal mediated. In women, it is closer to 45% which means that even if the hormones are perfectly balanced, ladies can be totally uninterested. Likewise, a woman can be very sexually responsive even though she has poor hormonal balance. Yes, I use a lot of hormones in my practice however I am careful to remind my patients that it is not a fix-all, silver bullet, fountain of youth answer.

We talked about erectile dysfunction (ED) in question 5.5. Phosphodiesterase-5 inhibitors like Viagra, Cialis and Levitra may help males with this problem. I have researched these meds for use in women and have found a modest increase in the literature for orgasm satisfaction when they took sildenafil (Viagra).[12] Caruso's group found that Sildenafil increased blood flow to the clitoris, suggesting that it may improve sexual functioning in much the same way it helps men.[13] There are many other medications that are promoted as sexual aids however there is very little quality medical literature that supports that. Some that you may have read about include: amantadine, bromocriptine, bethanechol, cyproheptadine, moclobemide, neostigmine and viloxazine. Interestingly, some Parkinsonism patients can become sexually more active and/or inappropriate. Many of the drugs that are supposed to increase sexuality are used in these patients (memantine, bromocriptine…) as well. So, is it a medication side effect or is it the disease? Until we have more information, I do not recommend these products. I think that research into similar dopaminergic drugs and their effect on human sexuality will be the wave of the future. Following the literature on phosphodiesterase pharmaceuticals (Viagra group of drugs), prostaglandins (particularly E1) and sympathomimetic drugs such as phenylethylamine will also be interesting.

Buproprion (Wellbutrin/Zyban) is commonly prescribed for sexual dysfunction. In studies, it was unlikely to cause a negative effect on sex and at least one study showed a modest improvement. When used alone, it works well as an antidepressant but sometimes I add it to another drug to minimize the prolongation of the plateau phase. Another plus to this med is that weight loss is often seen.

Rarely, Trazodone (Desyrel) can cause priapism. This is a prolonged and painful erection. It can cause permanent erectile dysfunction (ED) so it needs to be treated urgently. I discuss this more in previous questions. Since only about 1 in 6000 men have this response to Trazodone, it can not be used primarily for ED.

Yohimbine (Yohimbe) is produced from the bark of an African tree. The literature supports improvement in erectile dysfunction in men. Nonetheless, we have had positive responses in many women. It is a prescription drug and has side effects; the most common includes fast heartbeat and an increase in blood pressure at the standard dose of 5.4 mg three times a day.

8.3 What medications can interfere with sex?

There are many pharmaceuticals that can negatively affect sexual functioning. Some are well know side effects while others are individualistic responses to these products. Remember that side effects can occur even in over-the-counter (OTC, non-prescription) medications, herbal preparations and illegal drugs as well. In terms of groups of medications, the antihypertensives, antidepressants, antipsychotics, narcotics, barbiturates, benzodiazepines, oral contraceptives and antihistamines are commonly felt to cause issues.[7] Side effects can include loss of sexual desire, loss of sexual response, prolongation of plateau phase and other orgasmic disorders, erectile disturbances, ejaculatory delay, retrograde ejaculation, fatigue, weight gain, change in sensory perception, priapism, agitation, vaginal bleeding, halitosis, physical pain, etc. Some of these effects have a direct and others indirect impact on sex. Ejaculatory failure or orgasmic failure as examples are direct effects. Weight gain and nausea can be considered indirect. Let's say that a medication causes muscle aches and pains as some anticholesterol medications do such as the statins (simvastatin[Zocor]). Since even hugging can be painful, you can see how sexual activity can be affected. Lunesta (eszopiclone) can bring on a nasty taste which can impact oral stimulation.

When people come in with these side effects, I usually have four options for them. We can reduce the dose, give them a drug holiday, add to the drug or change the drug. Sometimes dropping the dose, even a little bit, can cure the problem. There seems to be a minimal drug level that sets off a side effect in certain individuals. If possible, we want to preserve the benefits while reducing the side effects. Additionally, the cost of the medication will likely also go down. While many tablets can be split, this is not the case in all. Ambien CR and Detrol LA are examples of extended release products that you should not try to cut in half. A drug holiday is when we stop the medication for a preset amount of time. It also decreases the blood levels which hopefully minimizes the adverse effect. This is something that you will want to do with the help of your provider. Each drug has its own pharmacokinetics. What may be potentially OK in one drug like fluoxetine (Prozac, Sarafem) can be deadly in another like some antiarrhythmic heart meds. As we talked about in the previous question, I will sometimes add Buprorion (Wellbutrin/Zyban) to another antidepressant when the original medication is working but the sexual side effects are a problem. I have seen this work on occasion. When all else fails and folks are still troubled by these issues and we can't seem to fix them, it is reasonable to change to another medication. Interestingly, changing to another similar drug even within the same category may fix the problem. Though sexual side effects are a "class effect" in SSRIs (fluoxetine, sertraline…), there can be a tremendous variation in how people respond to these drugs.

A few notes about pharmaceuticals. When we do drug research, we ask study participants (volunteers) about AEs. These Adverse Events are then tabulated and the more common ones are eventually listed in the product information material. Sometimes, there is an AE which, though serious, has nothing to do with the drug. A few years ago, I was involved in a study where a woman was ultimately found to have a cancer after starting the medication. It was obvious to me that she probably had this malignancy for many years before she even came to us. However, it was coded as a serious AE.

Here is another example of how things can be misinterpreted. The side effects listed for many sleep aid drugs include fatigue and somnolence. It seem silly to list the desired effect as an AE but that is how the system works. So, if you are too tired to have sex after taking Lunesta (eszopiclone), that medication can be listed as interfering with sexual functioning. Other thoughts: there are folks who respond paradoxically to certain meds. Many people take diphenhydramine (Benedryl…) for sleep (it is the active ingredient in many other-the-counter sleep aids). Yet there are other people in whom the medication boosts them too much to the point of causing agitation.

Here is an example of when a side effect is not one

really. I started a young woman on Ritalin for Attention Deficit/HyperActivity Disorder (ADHD). Ritalin is much more likely to cause an enhancement in sexual functioning rather than the opposite so I was surprised when she mentioned that she was having such problems on her follow up appointment. It turned out that she actually responded so well and her self-confidence improved so much that her boyfriend was having a hard time adjusting to his "new" girlfriend which upset their love making pattern. More thoughts regarding medication side effects. When you read that drug X is associated with decreased libido, keep in mind that only a certain percentage of people have this effect. Usually, the majority never have a problem. I have also seen that some folks develop a side effect to a medication only after I tell them about the potential for that side effect. In other words, they may find that problem only after they expect to develop it. I have patients who refuse to read the product information sheet because they recognize that they will tend to look for the side effects in themselves. Finally, we usually test drugs in relation to a placebo or inert product. This tells us if the drug is working and helps us figure out the side effects. However, there are a large number of side effects that people report while on no drug at all. The moral of the story here is that you need to understand drugs in the context of where the information is coming from. Be aware of possible issues but remember that you are an individual with your own response to the meds. And if a product is described as having NO side effects then I would be extra skeptical. Even taking too much water can have side effects like a low sodium level and an increase in urinary frequency.

    Anecdotal evidence is particularly effective at influencing human behavior. If someone takes a product and describes in glowing terms how it helped them with their sexual problem, you may find that you identify with that person. You may be tempted to try the product that the person, who may be an actor or paid to say whatever you read, is promoting. Keep in mind who benefits from the use of the product. For example, the company promoting the "only" or "real" or "original" formulation will make money on your gullibility or desperation. I get very concerned when patients come in with a bag full of products that they bought online or locally on the advice of a friend or advisor. Usually, these sad folks spent a large sum of money without doing their homework; they relied on hearsay, anecdotal evidence and blind trust. One lady I know brought in a box with about $900 of Chinese preparations that her naturopath sold her. It was clearly not working for her and she certainly could not afford that kind of expense.

On the following pages, I have put together a list of many but not all medications that can have sexual side effects.[15]

Medication/names	Sexual side effects
Antihypertensives	
Atenolol	impotence
Bethanidine	reported
Chlorothiazide	impotence
Chlorthalidone	reported
Clonidine	impotence, ejaculatory dysfunction
Doxazosin	impotence, ejaculatory dysfunction, priapism
Enalapril	impotence
Guanabenz	reported
Guanethidine	impotence, ejaculatory dysfunction
Guanfacine	impotence
Hydralazine	reported
Hydrochlorothiazide	sexual dysfunction
Labetalol	ejaculatory dysfunction
Lisinopril	impotence
Methyldopa	impotence, decreased libido
Metoprolol	impotence, decreased libido
Minoxidil	reported
Nifedipine	impotence
Phenoxybenzamine	ejaculatory dysfunction
Phentolamine	priapism
Prazosin	ejaculatory dysfunction
Propranolol	impotence, decreased libido
Reserpine	impotence, decreased libido
Spironolactone	impotence, decreased libido
Terazosin	ejaculatory dysfunction
Thiazides	impotence
Triamterene	reported
Verapamil	impotence

Psychiatric Medications

Amitriptyline	impotence, ejaculatory dysfunction
Amoxapine	impotence, decreased libido
Buspirone	reported
Clorazepate	reported
Chlordiazepoxide	decreased libido
Chlorpromazine	ejaculatory dysfunction
Chlorprothixene	ejaculatory dysfunction
Desipramine	ejaculatory dysfunction
Diazepam	reported
Doxepin	impotence, ejaculation dysfunction
Fluoxetine	orgasmic disorder
Fluphenazine	ejaculatory dysfunction, decreased libido
Haloperidol	ejaculatory dysfunction
Imipramine	impotence, ejaculatory dysfunction
Isocarboxazid	ejaculatory dysfunction
Lithium	impotence
Lorazepam	decreased libido (all benzodiazepines)
Maprotiline	ejaculatory dysfunction
Meprobamate	reported
Mesoridazine	ejaculatory dysfunction, decreased libido
Nortriptyline	ejaculatory dysfunction
Oxazepam	reported
Perphenazine	ejaculatory dysfunction
Phenelzine	ejaculatory dysfunction, decreased libido
Prochlorperazine	decreased libido, ejaculatory dysfunction

Protriptyline	impotence, ejaculatory dysfunction
Risperidone	sexual dysfunction, impotence, ejaculatory dysfunction
Thioridazine	ejaculatory dysfunction, decrease libido, priapism
Thiothixene	ejaculatory dysfunction, impotence
Tranylcypromine	ejaculatory dysfunction
Trazodone	priapism
Trifluoperazine	ejaculatory dysfunction
Triflupromazine	ejaculatory dysfunction

Other medications

Alcohol	impotence, testicular shrinkage
Aminocaproic acid	reported
Amphetamines	impotence, libido changes
Antiandrogens	impotence
Atropine	reported
Barbiturates	reported
Benztropine	reported
Biperiden	reported
Bromocriptine	reported
Busulfan	reported
Carbamazepine	impotence
Cimetidine	decreased libido, impotence
Clofibrate	impotence
Cocaine	reported
Codeine	reported
Cyclobenzaprine	reported
Cyclophosphamide	reported

Cyproterone	Decreased libido, impotence, reduced ejaculatory volume
Diacetylmorphine	reported
Digoxin	reported
Dihydrocodeine	reported
Dimenhydrinate	reported
Disopyramide	reported
Disulfiram	impotence
Estrogens (Premarin, Prempro…)	impotence, low libido
Famotidine	reported
Fentanyl (and derivatives like ohmefentanyl)	low ejaculatory volume, impotence, low libido
Finasteride	impotence, decreased libido, low ejaculation volume
Furazolidone	reported
Gemfibrozil	impotence
Goserelin	low libido
Heroin	low libido
Hydrocodone	reported
Hydromorphone	reported
Hydroxyzine	reported
Indomethacin	reported
Ketoconazole	reported
Levodopa	priapism
Licorice	reported
Luprolide	low libido
Marijuana	reported

Meclizine	reported
Meperidine	reported
Methadone	reported
Metoclopramide	impotence
Morphine	reported
Nicotine	reported
NSAIDs	reported
Omeprazole	impotence
Orphenadrine	reported
Opiates	reported
Oxycodone	reported
Oxymorphonephenytoin	reported
Prochlorperazine	ejaculatory dysfunction, impotence, priapism
Procyclidine	reported
Propantheline	impotence
Propoxyphene	reported
Promethazine	reported
Ranitidine	reported
Simvastatin	impotence
Trihexyphenidyl	reported

8.4 I hear that blood pressure medications can mess things up for me. What medications should I worry about?

Like antidepressants, antihypertensives are commonly implicated in sexual side effects. These include the ones in question 8.3. In addition, people with elevated blood pressure may be overweight and have hardening of the arteries both of which can affect sexual functioning. Weight loss and exercise are two interventions that may improve things sexually. After a while, you may also find that you won't need to take medications either. I often tell my patients that most diseases can be improved with exercise and that obesity has has no benefit on functioning except for cold environments like frigid lakes.

8.5 I'm not an alcoholic however I noticed that sex is much better after a drink or two. Dr. Laury, is this normal?

Alcohol has been called the "social lubricant" for good reason. Among its many effects, it tends to disinhibit people. This can work to your advantage if you have performance anxiety, for example. Let's say that you have a tendency towards spectatoring (question 3.8) and you worry about how you look or act during sex. Alcohol may help you here. However, moderation is the key. As you know, alcohol can also reduce good judgment. Inebriated people for millennia have made poor decisions that have had serious impacts on their lives. These include everything from STIs, rape, car accidents, theft and loss of memory to waking up next to the wrong partner. These impacts can affect people emotional, financially, medically or professionally for the rest of their life. In males, alcoholism can cause gynecomastia (breast development), obesity, testicular shrinkage and ED. Generally, I recommend no more than one drink on average per day for women and two for men. I become concerned when someone downs more than 3 to 4 drinks at one sitting. Alcohol is a two edged sword. It may help things along when done in control and it can come back to bite you under the wrong circumstances. Yes, I have many patients who use alcohol to improve their sex life however I would much prefer for them to figure out why they feel the need for the alcohol in the first place. With that information, they can enjoy things authentically.

8.6 Is there any truth to aphrodisiacs?

Throughout history all sorts of products have been used; most without benefits. These products are supposed to stimulate sexual desire, decrease sexual inhibition, prolong sexual potency or inflame genital tissues. Some of these medications can be not only illegal, but can be deadly such as giving someone narcotics or Rohypnol (flunitrazepam) in order to coerce them into having sex. Some are irritating to the urinary and genital structures like capsaicin (chili pepper) or "spanish fly" (cantharides). Herbal preparations may contain *Turnera microphylla* (Damiana), *Piper methysticum* (Kava), *Epimedium sagittatum* (Horny goat weed) or *Tribulus terrestris* (Puncture vine). Other ingredients used around the world include Rhinoceros horn (a major reason for the poaching of these animals), chocolate, asparagus (phallic shape?), peppers, dog blood, fish bile and oysters (clitoral shape?). There is no good evidence that these work reliably. Remember that about 30% of the time, these products will work just based on the placebo expectation effect. So even if it worked for your friend, it may still be a worthless expense for you.

Exercise may help prevent ED. I have seen studies noting improvement of about 30%.

Ptychopetalum olacoides also known as potency wood is pushed as a sexual aid. Very little information is known about this tree. The one study that I found suggested minimal, short term effects on rabbit penises. How this applies to human ones is questionable.

Withania somnifera (Ashwagandha) is occasionally promoted

for sexual issues. I found that there is a lot of literature looking at this supplement in relation to cancers, dementia and sleep but not for sexual problems. At this point, I don't recommend it to my patients or their partners.

Maca (*Lepidium meyenii*) may ultimately be of use for ED but for right now, no good literature supports it. There is one mouse study by Zheng and his group that shows promise however I would venture to guess that no mice are reading this book.

Vitamin E is an interesting supplement. In Peyronie's disease (see question 4.3) there has been some improvement with Vitamin E supplementation. Since PD is associated with erectile dysfunction and Vitamin E is associated with PD some have linked the two and voila, a new treatment for ED is born. Does it work? I found very little information to that effect and even when it showed improvement, the Vitamin E was often combined with other products complicating the picture. My take: take it with caution as it thins the blood and use it with a fair degree of skepticism.

You may see some information on Zinc and sexual dysfunction. Zinc deficiency is probably related to ED particularly in the obese, hypertensive or kidney disease patients. However, and this is the important point, zinc supplementation is not likely to improve sexual functioning in these or even normal zinc level men. Like many supplements, the literature is sparse but the hype is not. Side effects exist with any product and zinc is certainly one of them.

DHEA (dehydroepiandrosterone) is often promoted for sexual dysfunction. I discuss this in the next question but it is worth mentioning it here as well. Lots of anecdotal information but not much hard evidence. Patients with sexual dysfunction tend to have lower blood levels of DHEA. In one Turkish study, Tekdogan found that DHEA levels increased when men with ED took Sildenafil (Viagra). This, however, doesn't necessarily mean that increasing DHEA improves ED. In fact, a Bulgarian paper felt that age related decreases in DHEA levels were not causative for ED but rather they suggested an increase in cholesterol was more likely (Tomova and Kumonov). If DHEA does help, then it may do so based on mood related improvement rather than a direct effect. Remember that DHEA converts to various hormones including estrogen and testosterone which is probably why it worked only in women in a pivotal trial.

Arginine is an amino acid which is involved in the production of nitric oxide (NO). NO participates in the relaxation of blood vessels which can lead to erections. In the research that I reviewed, I found little to no benefits of arginine by itself but a fair amount of benefit when it was supplemented by other products like Yohimbine. Keep on watching the literature, right now I don't recommend it as a potent sexual aid but it has potential for both genders once we understand more how to use it.

Korean Red Ginseng, also called Asian ginseng (*Panax ginseng*), has been used throughout history as an aphrodisiac. In the November 2002 Journal "Urology", a quality study was described where men with Erectile Dysfunction were helped with 900 mg given three times a day. There is some information that suggests that it may benefit women as well however it does act as a mild estrogen like compound so breast and uterine cancer patients should be aware of this. It can also cause thinning of the blood. Be careful with falls. Sometimes the ginseng that is sold is actually a different plant (Siberian ginseng [*Eleutherococcus senticosus*]) or a similar but less effective relative (American ginseng

[*Panax quinquefolius*]).

Ginkgo biloba: after reviewing the medical literature, I find that some studies show some improvement for ED and other sexual dysfunction in males and females. However, in the better designed studies (i.e. placebo controlled, double-blinded), there was no difference between the sugar pills and gingko. People may argue about dosing, concentration, etc. but based on this info, I would not promote this herbal. It may be better at thinning the blood but this can be a problem if folks fall or are accident prone.

People sometimes ask me "What is the harm of taking some of these products even if there is only a placebo effect?" First, you still spend money on worthless items. Your purchase supports an industry that thrives on pseudoscience and taking advantage of people. You are taking something that doesn't work instead of taking a real product. Even placebos have side effects and can interact with other medications....

8.7 Does DHEA really help?

DHEA has been touted as the miracle hormone but without much supportive evidence. Depending on who you read, it is supposed to improve skin thickness, reverse aging, help lose fat, slow down brain aging, reduce cancer risk, increase muscle and elevate the sex drive. It is interesting that much of the hype refers back to one major study done on DHEA over 12 years ago. In the original Morales paper, there was no increase in libido and male hormone increase was mainly seen in women.[14] Despite this, males have to be especially careful with the dosing since in theory it can negatively affect the prostate. Breast cancer issues are also a concern for women. The women who take it on their own often complain of irritability and agitation. In summary, we know very little about this product and therefore taking it amounts to self-experimentation.

9
Hormonal, Systemic, and Medical Issues

9.1 I am a 75 year old man with type 2 Diabetes. What can I do about fixing my sex life?

You didn't mention just what the problem was so I'll start by using the common ones. Diabetes comes in two main flavors; the rare one is Diabetes insipidus and other is Diabetes mellitus (also called sugar diabetes or simply DM). DM also has two main types: Type 1 and Type 2. As people age, there is a predominance of Type 2. You may also see it called Insulin Independent Diabetes or Non-Insulin Dependent Diabetes. This is a major health care issue as the American Diabetic Association (ADA) states that it affects 7% of Americans. One theory for all the myriad medical problems that occur is that the excess sugar causes (somehow) harm to the microvasculature in the body. This means that blood vessels are injured, leading to damage to the organ served by those vessels. DM affects the eyes (leading to cataracts and blindness), kidneys (leading to failure and dialysis), feet (leading to loss of balance, feeling and blood flow which can mean sores that don't heal and, eventually, amputations) and, of course, the genitals. When penile blood flow is reduced, impotence can occur. Erectile dysfunction (ED) can occur up to five times more commonly. The good news is that, sometimes, good glucose level control may help this situation. The not so good news is that if there is ED and the sugar leves are already optimally controlled, then the ED is not likely to get better. Fortunately, there are options for you (see question 5.5).

Just another plug for exercise: there is almost no disease that is not helped by an appropriate amount of exercise. Remaining active can help some folks' sex life tremendously. Benefits can include more stamina, weight control and improved self-esteem.

9.2 My husband has had a stroke. We are being creative in terms of our love making but will sex hurt him?

There a two main types of stroke: hemorrhagic and the more common, ischemic one. Stroke is associated with high blood pressure so the major concern is: "Does sex increase blood pressures enough to increase the risk of another stroke?" There is no good research that shows that sex causes strokes. Furthermore, there is no good research that shows that sex after a stroke can worsen the disease. However, stroke can affect sexual functioning both directly and indirectly. The sexual organs may lack normal sensation and may not function adequately for intercourse. It is fairly common for women to have vaginal dryness after a stroke and for male to have erectile problems. This means that certain sexual activities may be difficult or impossible after a portion of the brain has been damaged. Partners may also be afraid of hurting or worsening a stroke victim leading to dysfunction.

Stroke victims may be very self-conscious about the way their body looks or responds. A common example is the drooping of half of the face or when a body part will just lay there; immobile. It may directly interfere with love making. Imagine trying to hug someone one armed or kiss someone who is constantly drooling. Problems with positioning can occur and must be accommodated. There are even couples who require a third person to physically arrange their bodies so that love making can occur. If you can't actually have intercourse, consider sensual massage, hugging and kissing. Some people find that they can enjoy their partner sexually even when they have no physical feeling in their genitals.

Fatigue is frequently seen which limits interest in having sexual relations. Not only can the tiredness affect the act of interacting with another human, it can also extend to the point that personal hygiene can be neglected. Exhaustion can be part of the disease process or it can be the result of medications that are taken as a result of the stroke. Please see the section on medications to see if your husband's medications are on the list. Because fine motor skills may be difficult, we may find that people don't get out of their pajamas, that they don't shave or put on makeup. This can turn off partners. Try to schedule sex when you both have more energy.

Psychologically, sexual closeness may involve shifting mental gears. There can be role reversals when one partner has a stroke. And think about the difficulty that some people would have in the following example: you just finished changing someone's diaper and now they want you to perform oral sex on them.

Another reason why people don't take care of themselves may because of depression. I address this in many sections of this book since it is a common medical problem and it often interferes with sexuality. Having a stroke is associated with depression. It is important to look for it when someone is having sexual issues.

Remember that stroke can affect the ability to speak so consider non-verbal communication. Many families have "secret" hand signals or codes that signal interest in doing things sexual. It is no different in couples who deal with stoke. Also, guiding someone's hand, for example, where you want contact can bypass speech. Emotional cues can be lost with strokes so communication may be tricky.

Another important point deals with informed consent. There may be loss of speech or competency. Therefore, it may be difficult to assess if someone can give permission to someone else to have sex with them. How do we know if they can say no to sexual advances? This is a big ethical issue that is still being intensively debated. Twenty years ago when I was working with mentally handicapped and emotionally disturbed individuals who lived in group homes, we didn't know if it was OK for them to have sex with each other. I still don't have the right answers for you at this time so stay tuned.

If there are incontinence issues, go to the bathroom before attempting sex. Put waterproof covers on the bed, have cleanup supplies immediately available. Women can tape up a catheter to their upper thigh and men have put a condom over a folded over catheter.

When dealing with stroke, I recommend that both partners discuss things honestly amongst themselves. You can still be affectionate but the methods may be different. Stop or change things if there is pain. Remain creative and enjoy!

9.3 I have arthritis and have found that sex in the evening is more difficult because of my pain. Do you have any other suggestions for me?

There are two main types of arthritis: osteo and rheumatoid. Arthritis is associated with inflammation of the joints so movement may be painful. Osteoarthritis (OA) is the most common form of arthritis and involves the breakdown of the cartilage between bones. The cause of OA is often not clear but Rheumatoid arthritis (RA) is felt to be related to an autoimmune response. This means that the body's own immune system attacks the joints and causes inflammation. Though there is much variation in individuals, RA tends to get worse in the evening as compared to OA which is worse in the morning. Therefore, I assume that you have RA. RA pain tends also to hurt more than OA's. Besides involving your health care provider, there are some things that you can do at home to improve sexual function. Many folks find that moist heat helps. Try to find time to get in a bath before (or during) sex. As I mention often, be creative; find those positions that are the most comfortable for both of you. Use pillows generously. Be flexible in terms of time of day. Consider massage before, during or after sex. Remember that sex and orgasm can help with pain by releasing your own pain control substances called endorphins as well as keeping your mind off of the discomfort.

9.4 How do I prepare for a doctor's visit?

I would encourage you to actually set up the appointment specifically to discuss sexual issues. Many patients bring in lists. I think that this is key as they may be rushed or anxious and forget something important. I also encourage you to bring in literature that you want to discuss. I often review internet and magazine articles that my patients bring in. Having a friend or partner come along with you also can help. A second person is very helpful at keeping some people focused and honest. If the provider starts talking "medicalese" and it is over the patient's head, stop them and have them rephrase things in a more understandable way. It serves no purpose if the practitioner "expounds eruditely on dyspareunia" if the patient doesn't understand a thing about the pain that she feels when they are having sex. Remember that an appointment is about you, the patient. If you don't get something, ask to clarify things. If you run out of time, set up another appointment. If you get a medication, find out about side effects, cost, expected benefits, when you should start seeing improvement, etc. Some people like to take notes as well. The most important advice is to just get into the office. Don't procrastinate to the point that you never make the visit.

9.5 What might I expect if I go to my doctor with sexual problems?

Every provider will do things a bit differently however, in my practice, we generally start with a questionnaire which covers a complete health history. We ask about conditions, medications, allergies, smoking, family history, etc. If there are "red flags", we might recommend more specific questioning, e.g. a depression, ADHD or bipolar survey (see examples in Appendix B). After review of this information, we sit down one on one and discussion your concerns in much greater detail; when the problem started, how it has impacted on functioning, the intensity, your concerns and, of course, your goals from treatment. This is where most of my information is gathered. Often the problem is obvious to me just by being a good listener.

A physical exam may be next. This is critical to pick up abnormalities that might be the cause of the problem. If I find a high blood pressure, this might suggest cardiovascular disease. There may be a large neck mass indicating thyroid disease. Another example would be noting thin, pale vaginal tissues which suggests a lack of estrogen, or seeing leakage of urine which can cause irritation to the tissues. Another might be finding abnormal spasm of the vagina (vaginismus, see question 3.3) that can cause intercourse pain. Atypical vulvar sensitivity might alert me to test for Diabetes or Multiple Sclerosis, both of which can cause sexual dysfunction including anorgasmia. Lab tests may be indicated depending on the findings. I might do a microscopic vaginal discharge smear where I could find evidence of infection or low estrogen effect. Blood tests might be ordered to look at thyroid (TSH, T3, T4…), diabetes (fasting glucose, hemoglobin A1C), prolactin, estrogen, progesterone and testosterone levels. Depending on the circumstances, I may need AM cortisol and DHEA levels, androstenedione or sex hormone binding globin levels.

Putting all of this together, we can often come to understand the problem and then offer some solutions to improve the situation.

9.6 I have Fibromyalgia and have to take narcotics to deal with the pain. Is it my imagination or has the medications decreased my sex drive?

Pain itself can impact on sexual functioning. Depression is also associated with chronic pain so there is another reason why you are losing your libido. Finally, narcotics tend to suppress the brain centers dealing with production of hormones. Typically, my patients on long term pain meds have very low levels of estrogens and testosterone. This is almost always associated with a reduction in libido. So as you can see, it is not your imagination at all. As an aside, patients with kidney disease also commonly have low testosterone. Interestingly, a kidney transplantation may reverse the side effects including erectile dysfunction. Part of treating fibromyalgia and depression involves prescribing exercise. This may also help with your libido issues.

9.7 Why is it that so many of my friends with medical problems have intimacy problems?

Each disease has its own effects on the body. Diabetes can cause all sorts of sexual dysfunction, many of which are related to damage to small blood vessels. High blood pressure also affects the vessels but also the treatment involves a number of medications that can interfere with sex (8.3). Parkinsonism is also associated with erectile dysfunction and abnormal sexual behavior. Hemophilia can cause extreme pain when blood vessels get clogged up with the patient's own abnormal cells. That clogging can also affect the penis leading to priapism and permanent damage. Arthritis can affect sexual activity also because of discomfort. There will be different reasons why diseases can interfere with sex and each disease may have a different reason why you may find sexual dysfunction. Sometimes it is the disease itself, sometimes it is the treatment. Speak to your provider. They may not have a clue that you are suffering with sexual problems, and they can't treat what they don't know about.

Another important consideration is that depression is very common particularly in chronic diseases. When someone is depressed, sex is typically negatively affected. Though we may not be able to cure the specific disease, by focusing on the depression the individual may find improvement in sexual functioning.

9.8 I was told that I have pelvic organ prolapse. How does that affect my ability to be sexually active?

Pelvic support issues are very common, particularly in women. You may hear it called by different terms such as cystocele, rectocele, dropped bladder, uterine prolapse, etc. Essentially, it involves problems with support of the pelvic structures. Things tend to fall down, fall out or otherwise get in the way. It is associated with pain, pressure, incontinence and difficulty urinating and defecation. It not usually associated with sexual problems. If a pessary (vaginal support product) is in the vagina, then yes, it can interfere with other things going in there. Also, if surgery has been done to repair the defects, sexual pain can be seen. Sex can actually make pelvic support problems better temporarily for a few reasons. Most women have sex horizontally meaning that they are on their back or front. This tends to reduce pressure transmitted to the vagina and thus the organs that are trying to fall down. Also, Kegel's that are done during sex may hold up organs temporarily. We know that sexual activity increases blood flow to the pelvis; this may improve tissue strength and give better support to structures.

9.9 I am incontinent. What suggestions do you have for me?

There are many different types of urine loss. If the problem is the overflow type where the bladder is so full of urine that leakage occurs, then draining the bladder before sex may help. People wearing a catheter may need to be more creative, e.g. remove the catheter, tape it up, work around it… There are some newer techniques now available to help people with retention by stimulating the nerves serving the bladder. This may allow some folks freedom from catheters. If the problem is urge incontinence, also called overactive bladder or OAB, where there is an overwhelming urge to void, there are many options. These may also include emptying the bladder before sex, medications, bladder retraining and biofeedback. The neural stimulator may also be useful in this type of incontinence. I have implanted Medtronic Interstim neurostimulators which really seem to help tremendously.

With intercourse, the bladder may be irritated leading to spasm which can worsen the symptoms of urgency and urine loss. I will reiterate that often when someone loses urine during sex, this can be very embarrassing however I often find that their partner is much less concerned about it. Plenty of folks have waterproof pads over their mattresses or just put down some towels. Don't assume that it will bother your partner. Communication is often the best way of dealing with this problem.

SUI or Stress Incontinence deals more with altered anatomy where an increase in abdominal and pelvic pressure causes urine loss. This is especially seen with orgasm. Again, empty before sex, consider medications (duloxetine), put a mattress pad down, be creative and enjoy yourself.

9.10 During my treatments for cancer, I found that my drive was gone. Will it come back?

The big three cancers in women are breast, lung and colon. Cancer therapy can include surgery, chemotherapy and radiation therapy. There are many side effects to the treatments that can affect you sexually. Nausea, fatigue, hair loss, diarrhea, scarring and pain are some common examples. After breast cancer sugery, the chest wall may be painful or, conversely, have no feeling at all. A woman or her partner may be uncomfortable looking at the chest. Sometimes, your partner may, out of concern for you, not approach you because they feel that it is "too early" to pursue things sexually. Vulvar cancer surgery may remove the clitoris which will affect things as well. The diagnosis of cancer brings on feelings of grief and loss. Denial, anger and depression are seen commonly and are considered normal. I will also see guilt in some cases. In counseling patients with cancers, I encourage good communication. No one can read your mind and you can not read other people's either. The best way around assuming anything is to talk to others about the situation. Many cancer victims actually don't need sex as much as cuddling and a supportive physical presence. There are also other ways to be sexual even without intercourse. Talk with your partner and find ways to enjoy each other's company.

9.11 During the treatment of vulvar cancer, the surgeon had to take a large amount of skin including my clitoris. Can I ever be sexual again?

Let's talk about sexuality for a moment. As you already know, sex is not just touching. Getting raped is not sexually stimulating yet the rapist may be doing exactly the same maneuvers that your lover may do in better circumstances. The answer to this lies in the brain's contribution to the act. Many women have had spontaneous orgasms without physical touch. Others can have a climax when non-sexual organs are caressed. This tells us that the brain is more important than the clitoris. Going through cancer as a survivor can be very emotional. Depression is common and there are grief issues to deal with. Body image problems can crop up as well. If you have a supportive partner, yes there is a good chance that you will continue to be sexual.

9.12 How do I find out my estrogen levels?

Since estrogens are very important for normal sexual functioning in women it is logical to know one's level. Most providers can order a simple blood test. Of note, I rarely test salivary estrogen levels any more. Some of the labs that my patients used were not up to the standards that I expected. In addition, saliva is produced in various concentrations and amount depending on hydration, feeding and even just thinking about food. Remember Pavlov's dogs where they trained them to drool just by ringing a bell? Finally, it can be a hassle to spit into containers multiple times and store saliva in the fridge.

Blood levels are easy to do but only reflect the amount of estrogens that are floating around at any one time. It doesn't tell us anything about how your tissues are using the hormone. I prefer, therefore, to rely on how my patients are responding based on their feelings. I can also test the target organs directly.

One simple office technique is the vaginal pH. This underutilized test checks vaginal secretions for acid/base levels. A normal "young" vagina runs around 4.5 (on the slightly acid side). A pH over 5 suggests infections and/or low estrogen levels. With this information, we can tailor therapy. I also take some of the swabbed material and look under the microscope for the maturity index. This involves evaluating how much effect estrogen actually has on the vaginal cells. These tests are painless and quick and may be very helpful in guiding therapy. Ask you provider to either do the test for you or refer you to someone who can.

9.13 Ever since my hysterectomy, I have gained a bunch of weight. And my friends did too. Why is that?

This is a common complaint. I have even heard it after my patients' cats have had their hysterectomy! So what is the deal here. At this time, modern medicine does not have a definite "why" but here are some good runner ups. Surgery usually involves pain, medications, a recuperation period and a list of restrictions. Many surgeons advise against exercise and strenuous activities right after an operation. Once a previously active women gets out of the habit of working out, it is often hard to return to that same level of exercise. It is somewhat of a self-fulfilling prophecy. Someone says that they haven't been able to exercise so they gain weight and lose strength only to complain that she can't work out because of the weight gain and weakness. Another reason deals with the way people create memories. A specific memory will often come with a link. People tend to remember things in context of something else happening; "when I was in college...", "after my third baby, I ...", "I gained weight right after my hysterectomy". Though the timing can be close, it may not be related at all.

Humans, in general, gain weight with the advancing years. You are likely to weigh more now than when you were a teenager and, therefore, linking this to the hysterectomy makes sense. Yes, your friends may have gained weight after their surgery but they would have gained weight even without it.

Hormones are often prescribed after hysterectomy, particularly when the ovaries are removed. Some of these are associated with weight gain. However, from the opposite perspective, there is literature that shows that even though ladies on hormone replacement gain weight, they actually gain less weight than if they did not take the estrogens and progesterones at all.

Depression can sometimes be seen after hysterectomy. It can be coincidental or related to reason why they had to have the uterus out in the first place. Cancer for example. Removing a woman's womb effectively sterilizes her; this can be quite emotional for some. Weight gain is associated with depression.

Bottom line: if there is weight gain after hysterectomy, check into all options before blaming the lost organ.

9.14 I noticed that many of my friends who are not sexually active, have gained weight. Does sex really burn that much calories?

You know, I have noticed the same thing with my patients. Reflecting on this, I do believe that sex burns a few calories but not enough to cause the difference we see. Talking to some of these ladies, I found that many had gained weight after they stopped having a partner that looked at them in the nude. If no one will appreciate all of the hard work that you have done to keep yourself in shape, then why bother? It is a somewhat pessimistic outlook on life, but it comes up often. On the other hand, I have plenty of patients who lost weight after a divorce. This seems more related to the ladies taking control of their lives and start being responsible for their health.

10
What to Do?

10.1 Are sex toys good or bad?

In the last ten years or so, we are recognizing that sexual toys may have health concerns. German chemist Hans Krieg found that many of the chemicals used in the products are present at a much higher level than we would like and are potentially toxic. In one study he found that phthalates outgassed in concentrations of over 200,000 parts per million whereas the allowable maximal daily dose was up to 3,000 ppm. At least in rats, studies showed that phthalates can be associated with testicular, renal and liver damage. Because of this information, there are laws in various countries regulating phthalates in children's toys. Laws governing sex toys may not be present so *caveat emptor*. Besides phthalate issues, diseases can also be transmitted when these items are shared so remember to clean the item thoroughly. You should know that latex is particularly hard to clean due to its porosity. Many people are sensitive or allergic to latex, especially health care workers where we see a 10% rate. Nonoxynol-9, a chemical spermicide, can also irritate sensitive tissues. Sugars are commonly found in lubricants and gels which may increase vaginal yeast infections. So what safe options are available? Glass, silicon and metal toys seem to be the safest.

10.2 I have been using a vibrator for many years. Is that a problem?

Issues that surround this question include: Can you get hooked on vibrators to the exclusion of real people sex? Can you permanently hurt yourself by using vibrators for an extended length of time? Does long term vibrator use reduce sensitivity of genital tissues?

There is no literature that I am aware of that shows that using vibrators or sexual toys can cause addiction. Some women use these more than others but the use of a vibrator doesn't, itself, cause addiction. What I think is happening when someone perhaps "overuses" their sexual toys involves psychological issues not physical ones. Clearly, it is easier to use an inanimate object than to go through the risk of STIs and rejection from a real person and you can take advantage of your toy at any time of day. It doesn't look like using a vibrator is the cause for an addiction but may instead be the outlet of a pre-existing addiction.

Permanent harm? Normal use of the vibrator is not likely to cause any long term issues. Inappropriate or excessive use can of course be a problem but this ought to be very rare. Some people are very sensitive to vibration in terms of numbness or hives but again, this should be the minority.

A decrease in sensitivity is also unlikely. We have, though, seen women who tend to have easier or exclusive orgasms with vibrators. Some of this may be psychological or neurological. For example, if you get used to firing up your little friend to have an orgasm and then sexual intercourse may not lead to the same outcome. I would recommend changing up your routine to keep things functional and interesting; let your partner use the vibrator on you or change the technique, etc.

10.3 Does exercise really help sexually?

Yes and for many reasons. Exercise increases blood flow to the brain which is associated with a feeling of well being and probably improves brain efficiency. In addition, you have heard about the "runner's high". Exercise can cause a release of the body's own "feel good" chemicals. These endorphins improve mood and reduce pain. As you can imagine, this can help sexually. Weight control involves exercise. If someone is in the normal body size range, sexual activity tolerance, self confidence and an increase in the number of potential partners is likely. Many chronic diseases are improved with exercise as well such as high blood pressure and diabetes, both of which can directly influence sexual function in a negative way. In addition, when the disease is under better control, people are less likely to need medications so there won't be drug side effects such as low libido and orgasm disorders. Finally, as the disease's physical changes reverse such as arterial plaque or osteoporosis, sexual functioning may improve.

A few notes on exercise. I recommend some exercise daily. Optimally, an hour a day of something physical is a good idea. This can include vacuuming, gardening, walking and yes, even sex. My healthiest patients all exercise and they alternate between different types. They may walk on Monday and Thursday, go to dance class Tuesday night, workout with weights Wednesday and Saturday, clean house on Sunday and take Friday off. When the weather is good they might golf, bike ride, do outdoors Tai Chi or swim. They don't overuse just one group of muscles and it keeps them more flexible. There is often a social component to their exercise and in addition, they tend to get less bored. Studies suggest that morning exercisers tend to stay with the activity longer than those who try to do it in the evening. Exercise in the morning tends elevate metabolism longer so you get more of the benefits of feelings of energy and weight loss for the same amount of work. One powerful technique that I am recommending more and more is the interval training. Low intensity, long duration exercise tends to make the body too efficient. It gets used to long walks for example and the benefits tend to decrease over time. High intensity, short duration exercise like extreme bicycling or fast running tends to fatigue the muscles, use up the energy stores like glycogen and cause the body to protect the fat stores instead of using them. Interval training involves alternating between higher and lower intensity exercise so the body doesn't get used to a set pattern. For example, if you are on a treadmill, you might start at 2 or 3 miles per hour on a flat surface for the first three minutes. Then, bump the speed up by 2 miles per hour and elevate the incline a few degrees for another 1 or 2 minutes. Follow that by again slowing things down for 2 minutes. The total workout time might only be 10 or 20 minutes but the effects last much longer. Give it a try. I have been impressed with the results in our patients.

Now the disclaimers. Check with your provider before starting any exercise routine, start slow, consider stretching before, warm your muscles before intense activity, wear the right clothing including correct shoes, walking is one of the safest types of exercise, etc.

10.4 What therapies are available to me for my sexual problems?

It really depends on your individual issue. Sometimes, education alone is enough to fix things, discussing things and debunking myths, learning about what is normal and reviewing variations. Other times, exercise, biofeedback or psychological therapy is indicated. Medications such as estrogen or testosterone may play a role. Surgery can be of use. Again, it depends on the specific issue that is found.

10.5 Talk to me about testosterone. Does it really work?

Testosterone is critical for male sexual functioning. Without it, the drive and performance suffers. In females however, hormones are much less important in terms of sexual activities. In other words, the hormones can be within normal limits but libido is zilch and vice versa. Remember that at this time testosterone is not approved for use in women for sexual dysfunction. Having said that, many practitioners (and I am one of them) use it selectively for certain women.

10.6 I went in to see my doctor and my visit wasn't covered under my plan and I got stuck with large bill. What is going on here?

Unfortunately, most codes that doctors use for sexual problems come up in the mental health category which can make it harder to get reimbursed. Here are some examples in the "Mental Disorders" group: premature ejaculation, female orgasmic disorder and hypoactive sexual desire disorder. If your insurance doesn't cover that category, you will end up paying more for that care. Some creative patients have found that if they come in with "menopausal symptoms" and "vaginitis" they get things covered. You might want to check with your insurance company before going in.

10.7 I want to become more comfortable with my body sexually but I am not comfortable with myself down there. What can I do?

Actually, this is very common. Daily, I hear from women that they don't understand why their partners are so interested in their female parts whereas the owners of such parts may find them "gross". Assuredly, there are differences in people's anatomical interests; there are "breast men" and "butt women". Generally, it is possible to desensitize a woman to the repulsion that they may have for their own anatomy. Various techniques are described that slowly allow more exploration (visually and physically) of their genitalia. These techniques may be continued until she feels pleasure in stimulation of her genitals which then is progressed until orgasm. I would recommend that she do the first part of this therapy alone, without interruption and in a safe environment. Ultimately, she may be able to transfer this ability to be comfortable with her body to her partner who may help by stimulating her in a similar fashion. There are books and groups available to help such folks.

10.8 Obviously we seniors were not brought up on the internet like the younger generation. Do we need this skill for today's sexual environment?

Clearly, you can still have sex the old fashioned way! The internet may however be of help. Here are some examples. Let's say that you are single and want to find a partner. You can talk to friends about your goals, go to events, call up previous partners, etc. Now, can also scan through hundreds of likely partners using a computer search. You might go to a website that specializes in people who like country music, dinner cruises or square dancing.

You could limit your list to Asian or Jewish singles if you wanted to. There are probably sites for one-legged, Portuguese, scuba-diving, Saskrit experts! Another use of the internet is for research. Say you want to go to go to the "best" restaurant in a large city. Instead of asking everyone for their opinion or buying a travel guide, you'll find that your homework is made easier by internet searching by city, cuisine, ratings or wine list. It can be useful to look up different senior trips or educational retreats.

Communication is very much a part of the computer world. Not only can you write a letter to someone electronically (email) but you can also send video clips, speak real time with someone else or video conference others.

Many of my seniors are a bit intimidated by the technology. I might suggest getting someone else to get you started or consider taking a course before jumping in with both feet. You may not even need to buy anything if you use a internet café or public library computer. It is a new world out there, so make it work for you!

11
Other Vaginal Issues

11.1 SOS! "Save Our Sex". My vagina is too loose.

Sometimes my job seems schizophrenic. In one exam room, I take care of a woman who has vaginal tightness that causes too much pain with intercourse. Then, I go next door and someone like yourself has the opposite problem. Vaginal laxity is often overlooked as a sexual problem however I find that it is fairly common. There are real and perceived issues. Yes, having babies and years of use can relax the vagina and the supporting tissues. It is unreasonable to expect that, after pushing an 8 pound baby through, the vagina will return to a predelivery state. Vaginal repairs after delivery can sometimes help and sometimes hinder normal vaginal function. I have seen some really botched repairs by someone up all night and who didn't really seem to care about the long term effects of their work. I have also seen some women in whom you couldn't tell that they had three babies come through. Admittedly, there are other reasons for good and bad healing including smoking, genetics, forceps deliveries, steroid use, etc.

Now for a physiology lesson. When a woman gets aroused sexually, the vagina will lengthen and lubricate. For many, this is why sex is not painful. As an example, in rape cases we will often see vaginal tears even if the perpetrator has a smaller penis than the lady is used to. Muscle strength also tends to decrease as we age, this includes the vaginal wall muscles. As men age they need more friction to maintain their arousal and, eventually, have an orgasm. If you put together the decreased vaginal tone, increased lubrication and increased penile frictional needs you can understand why we hear more looseness complaints as the couple ages.

What to do? Kegel exercises, if done right, are of value. They can reduce stress urinary incontinence, improve vaginal tone, improve quality of orgasm for both genders and reduce the need for future pelvic surgery. The main problem is that the majority of women learn the Kegel's incorrectly. During a pelvic exam, I will often ask a woman to tighten those muscles to determine if it is done right. I usually start with imagery. I might say something like "Close you eyes and pretend that you are on the toilet urinating. Now, all of the sudden, someone rushes in and you need to immediately stop the flow of urine." With my abdominal hand, I assess whether the belly muscles remain soft. My vaginal hand will tell me if the correct muscles are working. By giving women feedback, we can often teach them to do the Kegel's right. The two main problems that I find include inappropriate tightening of the abdominal wall muscles and weak vaginal contractions. Electronic biofeedback can also be helpful. We will occasionally use physical therapists to help with pelvic support issues. It may actually be covered by insurance! Some ladies buy all sorts of products that promise better sex, better muscle control and less incontinence. There are many different approaches to vaginal tightening exercises. There are weights, spring loaded gadgets, metal bars, fluid filled pressure units, biofeedback strain gauges, etc. Do your homework first. Remember that your goal may be different than the company's. Which one is the best? I feel that the one that you will use and the one that will tone the correct muscles. I personally tend to favor the vaginal weights for my patients. They come in a set. The routine is to start with the lightest one, place it in the vagina and while standing, try to keep it from falling out. Most of my patients use it in the shower. Gradually, increase the weight. We had one overachieving lady for whom I had to build metal weights because she graduated through all of the "regular" ones!

Another option for some will be surgery. I am commonly asked to tighten the vagina at the time that I do other pelvic surgery. If this is something that you are thinking about, make sure that your surgeon has the experience and you have the correct expectation regarding the surgery. I have seen plenty of poor outcomes in ladies who then come to me with problems. What about all those vaginal cosmetic surgeries that you may have heard about? Generally, like all cosmetic procedures, the satisfaction is related to expectation. Just like breast implants or nose shaping, people need to understand that we are improving that body part. We are not fixing the psychological make up of the person, their insecurities and the social issues. I spend a lot of time with ladies regarding this issue. Yes, I can change the shape of the vagina but I can't fix the marital situation at home. A psychologist or counselor can often be of great benefit.

11.2 I found a honey but I am afraid that it has been so long that there are cobwebs up there. What can I expect if we get physical?

In all honesty, things haven't changed that much from your younger days. The courting phase is similar though you might get your love letters by email and the flowers delivered by courier came from Peru. If and when you plan on getting sexual you might be pleasantly surprised by the improvements brought on by time. Usually, communication is improved, disinhibitions are reduced and love making skills are better developed. Your preferences are likely to be respected so it is important to clearly identify potential issues. You might say, for example: "It has been so long since I have had sex, I need you to go slow." or "Even pelvic exams cause a lot of pain and bleeding so please be patient with me. I want this to work for both of us." I just don't hear that kind of intimate communication with my 20 year old patients.

You may want to actually make an appointment with your provider as many women in my practice do before becoming intimate. I may suggest some options, prescribed some medications or fix something that would have otherwise interfered with your sexual plans. Last week I saw a lady who has some vaginal scarring that had caused sexual pain. I have her set up for in-office repair and I am sure that things will be improved. The week before, I did a labioplasty where I removed extra labial tissue that would get in the way of sex. I teach ladies about lubricants, the importance of foreplay and do a little discussion on STIs.

11.3 My pubic hair is thinning. Is this normal?

Losing pubic hair is common as people age. Pubic hair initially grows in response to your puberty hormones. As folks age, there are drops in hormones. In women particularly, there is a significant reduction of estrogen and testosterone which probably is responsible for the thinning and eventual loss of pubic hair. Hair loss can occur due to other hormonal imbalances like thyroid dysfunction. Obviously, waxing over time as well as laser hair removal may thin hair on purpose. Radiation and chemotherapy can affect hair growth. Nutritional deficiencies can also be at fault.

Not surprisingly, there are now pubic hair transplant surgeons willing to help in that department.

12
The Dangers of Sex

12.1 Tell me truthfully Dr. Laury. How safe is sex at my age? I am 68.

That is a fascinating question. When my patients ask me that it usually means that they have been out of the game for a number of years. They are generally asking about sexually transmitted infections. STIs do occur at any age. These include Hepatitis, AIDS (since 1995, the number of AIDS patients over 50 has quintupled according to The Centers for Disease Control and Prevention), Chlamydia, Gonorrhea and Syphilis among others. Though there tends to be less promiscuity as we age, one hears of multiple cases of STIs in nursing homes which are probably related to one infected client who is making his or her way around the facility. In addition, condom use and STI testing is much less common in the older population

Sexual predators are a problem. If you have money, are alone, are lonely or have some degree of mental incapacity this may attract sexual predators. We talked about Elder abuse in question 6.1 which certainly includes Elder rape. Date rapes occur at any age. The ugly truth is that one woman in eight will be forcibly raped at some point in their life. Sexual abuse is in the range of up to 50% depending on who you read.

The internet has generated a new set of dangers including identity theft and financial scams. Many people on fixed incomes hope to improve their monetary situation and fall prey to these scams. Seniors are a favorite target. People have been known to lose their entire retirement savings in these scams. Be careful!

Emotionally, the same benefits and dangers are present that one would expect at any age. Depression is very prevalent in our society. Risk factors include being female, loss of social support, previous history of depression and persistent stressors. Being rejected by someone can be difficult. Interestingly, some research suggests that the fewer the partners available, the better they look.

On physical exams, I find vaginal tears fairly often. Vaginal and bladder infections are quite common.

Though it looks like a lot of negatives, truthfully, relationships (sexual and other) are very rewarding. I am just trying to instill some caution into the mix. Another positive: I have never seen an unintended pregnancy after the age of 50.

12.2 I have had a hysterectomy. Will I get sexual infections if I start using my "playground"?

This question comes up fairly often since about 30% of women have hysterectomies by age 60. Yes, you can still get most of the STIs. It will not however progress to give you a uterine or tubal infection since those parts are gone. Herpes, AIDS, Hepatitis and a bunch of other nasties can still be transmitted. The use of condoms is unfortunately low in seniors but should be promoted. So have fun but do it responsibly.

12.3 I have some, let us say, eclectic tastes sexually so I have to go through some alternative websites and groups to find appropriate partners. Is this bad?

We have plenty of patients who have unique or unusual sex interests. Somehow, they tend to find others with similar kinks. How? I am not completely sure. At least locally, we don't have S & M parties and Latex Anonymous groups that I know about. Some sexual practices can be dangerous – sexual asphyxition or autoerotic asphyxiation, for example, involves cutting off blood and oxygen flow to the brain when near orgasm. Unfortunately, up to 1000 people suffocate and die a year in the US this way and many are permanently brain damaged. Sexual cutting, piercing and mutilation can cause scars, infections and pain. All sorts of objects have to be retrieved by physicians when they "accidentally" get lodged in body cavities. I recall counseling a woman to consider an alternative device for masturbation rather than garden fresh cucumbers because the spines were potentially irritating to her tissues.

So be careful with the techniques as well as the technician. Besides the direct effects from certain sexual practices, I am concerned that you may attract a predator rather than a supportive partner.

Post-script

Writing this book was lots of fun. It was also a big responsibility; the information that I presented had to be accurate yet legible. I needed to balance scientific writing with a light hearted approach to a very sensitive subject. Acutely, I felt the weight of accountability to my medical profession. I reveled in the joy of bringing together a cohesive package of knowledge from out of the chaos of information, misinformation, scams, myths and traditions that I encountered. I learned so much more than I anticipated. As in most of my education, I came to appreciate that the more I advanced my own knowledge, I realize that there is much more to learn. I sincerely hope that this book can positively impact those spirits out there who continue to enjoy life and it's rich rewards.

13
Resources

Dating Services More Specifically for Seniors:

www.seniorfriendfinder.com
    (couldn't find any age minimum)
www.seniorpeoplemeet.com
www.maturedatelink.com
    (seems more sexual rather than interpersonal)

Dating Services non-specific for Seniors:

www.eharmony.com
www.friendfinder.com
www.ge-dating.com (great expectations)
www.match.com
www.perfectmatch.com
www.personals.yahoo.com

Organizations such as the American Cancer Society (Schover, 1988), the United Ostomy Organization, and the National Jewish Center for Immunology and Respiratory Medicine have published excellent brochures on maintaining sexual function in the face of specific medical illness.

Travel Resources:

Elder hostel
www.elderhostel.org
11 Avenue de Lafayette | Boston, MA 02111
1(800) 454-5768

Eldertreks
www.Eldertreks.com
1 (800) 741-7956
adventure@eldertreks.com

Grand circle travel
www.gct.com
1 (800) 321-2835

Leisure Care, LLC
www.leisurecare.com
1601 Fifth Avenue, Suite 1900
Seattle, WA 98101
(206) 325-7827

Accessible Journeys
www.disabilitytravel.com
35 West Sellers Avenue
Ridley Park, PA 19078
1 (800) 846-4537

Seniors Contacts:

AARP
601 E Street NW
Washington, DC 20049
1-888-OUR-AARP (1-888-687-2277)

Gray Panthers National Office
1612 K Street, NW
Suite 300
Washington, DC 20006
1 (800) 280-5362 or (202) 737-6637
Fax: (202) 737-1160
info@graypanthers.org

National Caucus on the Black Aged (NCBA)
1220 L Street NW Suite 800
Wash, DC 20005
(202) 637-8400
www.ncba-aged.org

Senior Action in the Gay Environment (SAGE)
305 7th Avenue, 16th Floor
New York, NY 10001
(212) 741-2247.
info@sageusa.org

Bibliography/References:

[1] Laumann, E. O., Paik, A., Rosen, R. C. (1999, February 10). Sexual Dysfunction in the United States: Prevalence and Predictors. *JAMA, 281*, 537-544.

[2] Marwick, C. (1999, June 16). Survey says patients expect little physician help on sex. *JAMA, 281*, 2173-2174.

[3] Melbourne women's midlife health project. Retrieved from www.psychiatry.unimelb.edu.au/midlife/index.htm

[4] Healthy Sexuality and Vital Aging: A Study by The National Council on the Aging, September, 1998. Retrieved from www.ncoa.org/attachments/SexualitySurveyExecutiveSummary.pdf

[5] Laury, G. (1977, March). Foreplay in Old Age. Med Aspects *Human Sex, 11*, 92-93.

[6] Glass, R. (1993). *Office Gynecology,* Fourth Edition. Baltimore: Williams and Wilkins.

[7] American College of Obstetricians and Gynecologists. (1999) *Precis: Primary and Preventative Care*, Second edition. Danvers: ACOG.

[8] Evans, R. W., Couch, R. (2001). Orgasm and Migraine. Headache: *The Journal of Head and Face Pain. 111(6)*,512-514.

[9] Lachs, M., Pillemer, K. (2004, October 2). Elder Abuse. *The Lancet*, 364, 1192-1263.

[10] Oswalt, S. B. et al. (2005, December). Sexual Regret in College Students. Arch Sex Behav. 34(6),663-669.

[11] Beers, M. Chapter 114, section 14. Merck Manual of Geriatrics, Third Edition, Online Update. Retrieved May 20, 2007, from http://www.merckmedicus.com/pp/us/hcp/framemm.jsp?pg=www.merck.com/mrkshared/mmg/home.jsp

[12] Claret, L. et al. (2006, August). Modeling and Simulation of sexual activity daily diary data of patients with female sexual arousal disorder treated with Sildenafil citrate (Viagra). Pharm Res, 23(8), 1756-1764.

[13] Caruso, S. et al. (2006, July). Changes in clitoral blood flow in premenopausal women affected by type 1 diabetes after single 100-mg administration of sildenafil. Urology, 68(1), 161-165.

[14] Morales, A. J., Nolan, J. J., Nelson, J. C., Yen, S. S. (1994, June). Effects of replacement dose of dehydroepiandrosterone in men and women of advancing age. J Clin Endocrinol Metab, 78(6), 1360-1367.

[15] Retrieved from epocrates, pdr, online, medline online, www.melbourneobserver.com.au/ob040811.pdf

Other Related References:

AARP/Modern Maturity (1999). AARP/MM Sexuality Survey-Summary of Findings. Retrieved December 4, 2000, from http://research.aarp.org/health/mmsexsurvey_1.html

Althof, S. E., Seftel, A. D. (1995). The evaluation and management of erectile dysfunction. Psychiatr Clin North Am, 18(1), 171-192. American Medical Association. Talking to patients about sex: Training program for Physicians.

Avis, N.E. et al (2000). Is there an association between menopause status and sexual functioning? Menopause, 7, 297-309.

Bachman, G. et al (2002). Female androgen insufficiency: The Princeton consensus statement on definition, classification, and assessment. Fertility and Sterility, 77(4), 660-665.

Basson, R. (2000). The female sexual response. A different model. Journal of Sex & Marital Therapy, 26, 51-65.

Berman, J.R., & Goldstein, I. (2001). Female sexual dysfunction. Urologic Clinics of North America, 28, 405-416.

Bem, D. (1965). An experimental analysis of self-persuasion. Journal of Experimental Social Psychology, 1, 199-218.

Crenshaw, T. L., Goldberg, J. P. (1996). Sexual Pharmacology: Drugs That Affect Sexual Function. New York: W.W. Norton & Co.

Davis, S.R. (2001, Summer). Testosterone treatment: Psychological and physical effects in postmenopausal women. Menopausal Medicine, 9(2), 1-6.

Dennerstein, L., Dudley, E. C., Hopper, J. L., Burger, H. (1997). Sexuality, hormones and the menopausal transition. Maturitas, 26, 83-93.

Diokno, A. C., Brown, M. B., Herzog, A. R. (1990). Sexual function in the elderly. Arch Intern Med, 150, 197-200.

Feldman, H. A., Goldstein, I., Hatzichristou, D. G. et al. (1994). Impotence and its medical and psychosocial correlates: results of the Massachusetts Male Aging Study. J Urol 151(1), 54-61.

Freedman, M. L. (1999). Assessment and Treatment of Erectile Dysfunction in Late Life. Presented at the American Association for Geriatric Psychiatry annual meeting. New Orleans; March 13.

Festinger, L. (1957). A theory of cognitive disonnance. Stanford, CA: Stanford University Press.

Festinger, L., Carlsmith, J. (1959). Cognitive consequences of forced compliance. Journal of Abnormal and Social Psychology. 58, 203-210.

Freedman, M. (2000). Sexuality in post-menopausal women. Menopausal Medicine. 8, 1-4.

Gitlin, M. (1994). Psychotropic medications and their effects on sexual function: diagnosis, biology, and treatment approaches. J Clin Psychiatry. 55(9):406-413.

Goodwin, A., Agronin, M. (1997). A Woman's Guide to Overcoming Sexual Fear & Pain. Oakland, Calif.: New Harbinger Publications.

Greenblatt, R.B. (1942). Hormone factors in libido. Journal of Clinical Endocrinology & Metabolism. 3, 305.

Hawton, K., Gath, D., Day, A. (1994). Sexual function in a community sample of middle-aged women with partners: effects of age, marital, socioeconomic, psychiatric, gynecological, and menopausal effects. Arch Sex Behav. 23:375-395.

Hällström, T. (1977). Sexuality in the climacteric. Clin Obstet Gynaecol. 4:227-239.

Kingsberg, S. (2000). The new (middle) age approach to female sexual dysfunctions [editorial]. Menopause. 7:286-288.

Koster, A., Garde, K. (1993). Sexual desire and menopausal development: a prospective study of Danish women born in 1936. Maturitas. 16:49-60.

Leiblum, S.R. (1991, October). The Midlife and Beyond. Presented at the 24th Annual Postgraduate Course of the Psychology Professional Interest Group of the American Fertility Society, "Sexual Dysfunction: Patient Concerns and Practical Strategies." Orlando, FL.

Lepper, M., Greene, D., & Nisbett, R. (1973). Undermining children's interests with extrinsic rewards: A test of the "overjustification hypothesis." Journal of Personality and Social Psychology. 28, 129-137.

Levine, S.B. (1998) Sexuality in Mid-life. New York: Plenum Press.

Levine, S.B. (1992). Sexual Life. New York: Plenum Press.

Metz, M., Miner, M. (1995). Male "menopause," aging, and sexual function: a review. Sexuality and Disability. 13(4), 287-307.

Renshaw, D. (1996). Sexuality and Aging. In: Comprehensive Review of Geriatric Psychiatry-II, 2nd ed. Washington, D.C.: American Psychiatric Press Inc.

Schiavi, R.C. (1999). Aging and Male Sexuality. Cambridge, UK: Cambridge University Press.

Schnarch, D. (1997). Passionate Marriage. New York: Henry Holt & Co.

Schover, L. R. (1988). Sexuality and Cancer. Atlanta: American Cancer Society.

Segraves, R. T. (1998). Antidepressant-induced sexual dysfunction. J Clin Psychiatry. 59(suppl 4), 48-54.

Spector, I., Rosen, R., Leiblum, S. (1996). Sexuality. In: Psychiatric Care in the Nursing Home. New York: Oxford University Press.

Web support and links:

About.com
www.womenshealth.about.com
Is There Sex after Menopause?

American Cancer Society
www.cancer.org/docroot/home/index.asp
Keeping Your Sex Life Going

Breastcancer.org
www.breastcancer.org
Sex and Intimacy

Cancer Research UK
www.cancerhelp.org.uk
Your Sex Life after Vaginal Cancer Treatment

Cleveland Clinic
www.clevelandclinic.org
Heart Surgery Recovery

DrDonnica.com
www.drdonnica.com
Menopause and Sex

Estronaut
www.womenshealth.org
Hysterectomy: Everything You Should Know

Health 24.com
www.health24.com
Does Recovering from Depression Mean Giving Up Sex?

Mayo Clinic
www.mayoclinic.com
Sexuality after Cancer Treatment: What Women can Expect

MedicineNet.com
www.medicinenet.com/script/main/hp.asp
Sex and Menopause

My Pleasure
www.mypleasure.com
Sexuality & Disability: History & Practice

National Cancer Institute
www.cancer.gov
Your Social Relationships after Cancer Treatment

National Kidney Foundation
www.kidneyhi.org
Sexuality and Chronic Kidney Disease

Netdoctor
www.netdoctor.co.uk
Sex after the Menopause

OBGYN.net
www.obgyn.net
The Basics of Gynecology – What Every Woman Should Know

Safe Menopause Solutions
www.safemenopausesolutions.com
Can Women Enjoy Sex after a Hysterectomy?

The Stroke Association
www.stroke.org.uk
Sex after Stroke

Third Age
www.thirdage.com
Sex after Menopause

WebMd
www.webmd.com
Breast Cancer Survivors: A Return to Sex and Intimacy

Yahoo Health
http://health.yahoo.com/topic/breastcancer
Breast Cancer: Sex and Sexuality

Glossary

Adhesions – scar tissue

Agglutinate – to cause to come together or unite, usually used in context where the vaginal lips seal together

Anhedonism – lack of interest in enjoyable activities

Anorgasmia – inability to have an orgasm

Antidepressant – something that helps improve or treat depression

Anus – the opening at the end of the intestinal tract where feces are passed to the outside

Anxiety – a state of tension or apprehension

Aphrodisiac – something that stimulates sexual interest or performance

Arousal phase – second part of the sexual response, involves physical and psychological responses to sexual stimulation

Arthritis – joint disease associated with inflammation

Asexual – without sexual urges or activity

Atrophy – the decrease in size or function of an organ, tissue or body part

Biofeedback – a technique that gives the user awareness of a body response to allow a change in that parameter. E.g. heart rate, temperature…

Cervix – the lower portion of the uterus. A rounded structure through which menstrual blood and babies may pass
Chordee – condition where the eret penis is bent
Chronic – of long duration
Climacteric – see menopause
Climax – see orgasm
Clitoris – small, sensitive, erectile, female organ located at the superior aspect of the vagina
Coital – having to do with sexual intercourse
Coitus – sexual intercourse
Corpora cavernosa – spongy penile tissue that allows for erections
Cystocele – protrusion of the bladder into the vagina

Defecation – the act of passing stool or feces
Depression – a mental illness that involves low energy, lack of interest, poor sleep, suicidal thoughts, etc. Thought to be associated with neurotransmitters such as serotonin
Desire phase – first part of the sexual response, involves the interest in being sexual
DM – Diabetes mellitus, "sugar diabetes"
DO – Doctor of Osteopathic Medicine
Dysmemurrhea – painful periods
Dysorgasmia – painful orgasm
Dyspareunia – painful sexual intercourse

ED – erectile dysfunction
Edentulous – with teeth
Ejaculation – the discharge of semen from the penis during climax
Email – "electronic mail". The transmission of information through electronic media like computers
Endometriosis – a complex syndrome involving pain, infertility, and an abnormally located endometrial lining
Endorphins – naturally produced chemicals that reduce pain or increase pleasure
Engorgement – swelling seen when an organ is filled with fluid
Enterocele – protrusion of the intestines into the vagina
Erectile dysfunction – failure to achieve an adequate erection
Erection – when the penis becomes firm due to blood flow to the organ

Feces – solid waste passed from the rectum
Female superior position – a sexual technique where the woman is on top of the male, usually sitting or squatting over him
Flatus – gaseous discharge from the rectum
Foreskin – tissue covering the tip of the penis
Fourchette – base of the vagina where the labia come together

Gay – homosexual, someone who is sexually attracted to the same gender
Genitalia – reproductive organs (usually the external visible ones)
Genitals – reproductive organs (usually the external visible ones)

Geriatrician – a medical doctor trained in the care of older patients
Glans penis – the head of the penis
GLBT – Gay, Lesbian, Bisexual, Transgender (variant of LGBT)
Gynecologist – a medical doctor specializing in female health issues
Gyneromastia – breast development in males

Hirsute – hairiness
Homosexual – someone who is sexually attracted to the same gender
HSDD – Hypoactive Sexual Desire Disorder
Hysterectomy – surgical removal of the uterus

IC - (see Interstitial Cystitis)
Impotence - generally used interchangeably with ED
Incontinence – involuntary loss of urine or feces
Infertility – the inability to achieve or complete a pregnancy
Interstitial Cystitis – syndrome consisting of feelings of urinary frequency and pain that is not infection related
Intercourse – sexual penetration of the vagina by a penis
IUD - InterUterine Device, used for contraception

Kegel exercises – muscle techniques used to improve vaginal tone

Labia – lips, usually pertaining to the vulva
Labia majora – the larger, thicker vaginal lips
Labia minora – the smaller, thinner vaginal lips
Labiaplasty – also spelled Labioplasty, plastic surgery to the vaginal lips usually done for cosmetic or reconstuctive reasons
Labioplasty – see Labiaplasty
Lesbian – a women who is sexually attracted to other women
Libido – "life instinct," generally associated with sexual interest
Lichen Sclerosis – a skin condition which involves itching as a symptom, pale tissues as a sign, often seen in the genital area.
LGBT – Lesbian, Gay, Bisexual, Transgender (variant of GLBT)
LS – see Lichen Sclerosis
Lubrication – secretions or liquids which decrease friction in the genitals

Mastectomy – surgical removal of a breast, usually because of cancer
Masturbation – self stimulation of the genitals for the purpose of enjoyment
M.D. – Medical Doctor
Menarche – when a woman starts menstuation
Menopause – when the ovaries stop functioning, see climacteric
Menses – regular shedding of the uterine lining
Menstruation – see menses
Migraine – type of painful headache
Mnemonic – memory aid
Multiorgasmic – repetitive orgasms

N.D. – Naturopathic Doctor
Neurotransmitters – chemical messengers that generally operate in the brain, e.g. serotonin, dopamine…

OAB – OverActive Bladder
Obesity – being significantly overweight
OCD – Obsessive Compulsive Disorder
Orgasm – a peak sexual experience associated with sexual organ contractions. Males also produce an ejaculation
OTC – over-the-counter
OverActive Bladder – a type of incontinence that involves bladder spasms
Ovary – hormone-producing female ovulating organ

Penis – male sexual organ used for urinating and sex
Pessary – vaginal device used to help support structures
Peyronies Disease – painful penile erectile condition associated with plagues
Pharmaceutical – dealing with drugs
Phirrosis – painful penile erectile condition associated with the foreskin
Plateau phase – third phase in the sexual response involving the maximal intensity of excitement. It is followed by Orgasm.
POP – Pelvic Organ Prolapse. Drop or extension of pelvic organs such as bladder and rectum into the vagina
Post coital – after sexual intercourse
Premature ejaculation – male orgasm reached prior to pleasuring his partner
Priapism – abnormal prolongation of an erection

Prostate – a male gland surrounding the urethra involved with secretions during ejaculation
Prosthesis – artificial body part
Pruritis – itching
Psychologist – a professional trained in the diagnosis, research and treatment of mental disorders
Psychiatrist – a medical doctor trained in the diagnosis and treatment of mental disorders
Pubococcygeus muscles – muscles attaching at the coccyx and pubic bone associated with vaginal support

Rectum – the lower part of the large intestine where stool is stored prior to defecation
Refractory phase – a time period where stimulation will not result in a male orgasm
Rectocele – protrusion of the rectum into the vagina
Reproductive organs – the body parts associated with a pregnancy, e.g. uterus, penis…
Resolution phase – after orgasm, bodily responses to excitement return to normal.

Scrotum – the sack that holds the testes
Serotonin – a neurotransmitter intimately associated with depression and anxiety
Sex – stimulation of the genital organs for the purpose of enjoyment
Sexuality – dealing with sex
Spasm – muscle contraction
SSRI – Selective Serotonin Reuptake Inhibitor. A type of antidepressant

STI – Sexually Transmitted Infection
Stress Urinary Incontinence – urine loss associated with coughing, sneezing, etc.
SUI – Stress Urinary Incontinence
Stool – feces
Syndrome – a disease of unknown cause

Testes – male sperm-producing organs
Testicle – often used interchangeably with "teste"
Testosterone – a hormone produced by both genders that is involved with muscle growth, sexual characteristics and response
TOT – Tension-free TransObturator Vaginal Tape procedure used to help incontinence
Transgender – an individual who feels that the sex assigned at birth is incorrect
TVT – Tension free Vaginal Tape used for incontinence procedures

Urethra – the tube that carries urine (and semen in males) from the bladder to the outside of the body.
Urethral meatus – the opening of the urethra where the urine (and semen in males) exits the body.
Urination – the act of passing urine out of the body
Urologist – a medical doctor specializing in disorders of the urinary system
Uterus – female organ where fetal growth occurs

Vagina – a tube-like female organ involved with sexual intercourse and birth

Vaginismus – a syndrome where the vagina involuntarily tightens making penetration difficult or impossible

Vasodilator – a substance that opens up blood vessels

Vestibulitis – a painful syndrome involving sensitivity of the vagina

Vibrator – an instrument that shakes rapidly usually used for stimulation of the sexual organs

Vulva – external female genitalia

Index

Adhesions	4.2
AIDS	12.1, 12.2
Agglutinate	8.2
Angina	4.3, 7.6
Antidepressant	8.2, 8.3
Anxiety	2.13, 3.7, 3.9, 5.5, 7.2, 8.5
Aphrodisiac	5.6, 8.6
Arousal phase	2.4, 3.1, 5.5, 11.1
Arthritis	2.2, 4.3, 5.9, 9.3, 9.7
Asthma	4.3
Atrophy	1.7
Biofeedback	10.4, 11.1
Bladder	2.6, 2.12, 3.3, 4.3, 4.4, 8.1, 9.8, 9.9, 12.1
Bridge technique	2.5, 3.7, 3.13
Buprorion	8.1, 8.2, 8.3
Candida	3.3
Cervix	4.3
Chordee	4.3

Climax	2.5, 2.6, 3.2, 3.17, 5.8, 9.11
Clitoris	2.4, 2.5, 2.12, 2.13, 2.17, 8.2, 9.10, 9.11
Coital	3.3, 4.4
Corpora cavernosa	4.3
Cystocele	4.3, 9.8
Defecation	9.8
Depression	1.7, 1.13, 3.1, 3.9, 3.11, 3.16, 5.4, 5.5, 6.2, 7.2, 7.7, 7.12, 9.2, 9.5, 9.6, 9.7, 9.10, 9.11, 9.13, 12.1,
Desire phase	2.4
Diabetes	3.4, 5.5, 9.1, 9.5, 9.7, 10.3
DM	9.1
Dyspareunia	3.3, 4.1, 7.9, 9.4
Ejaculation	2.6, 2.12, 2.13, 3.10, 4.3, 5.5, 5.7, 5.8, 8.1, 8.2, 8.3, 10.6
Email	1.14, 10.8, 11.2
Emphysema	4.3
Endometriosis	3.3, 4.1

Endorphins	4.2, 9.3, 10.3
Enterocele	4.3
Erectile Dysfunction	5.5, 8.2, 8.6, 9.1, 9.6, 9.7
Erection	2.4, 2.6, 2.7, 2.12, 3.3, 3.13, 4.3, 5.5, 5.6, 5.8, 5.12, 8.2, 8.6
Estrogen	2.7, 2.12, 2.17, 3.3, 3.6, 3.12, 3.13, 3.15, 4.1, 4.4, 7.1, 7.11, 8.2, 8.6, 9.5, 9.12, 9.13, 10.4, 11.3
Genitals	2.5, 8.2, 10.7
Geriatrician	1.6
Glans penis	5.8
GLBT	2.14
Gynecologist	1.6
Gynecomastia	8.5
Hemophilia	9.7
High Blood Pressure	9.2, 9.5, 9.7, 10.3
Hormone	2.7, 2.12, 2.16, 2.17, 3.1, 3.6, 3.9, 3.16, 4.1, 8.2, 8.6, 8.7, 9.5, 9.6, 9.12, 9.13, 10.5, 11.3

HSDD	3.1, 3.14
Hypertension	2.2, 5.5
Hysterectomy	3.16, 9.13, 12.2
Impotence	5.5, 5.6, 8.3, 9.1
Incontinence	5.9, 9.2, 9.8, 9.9, 11.1
Infertility	1.8
Internet	1.2, 5.3, 9.4, 10.8, 12.1
Introital Dyspareunia	3.3, 4.1
Interstitial Cystitis	3.3, 4.4
IUD	3.3, 4.3
Kegel exercises	3.12, 9.8, 11.1
Labia	2.17, 11.2
Lesbian	2.3, 2.14, 5.2, 7.9
Libido	5.4, 5.6, 8.3, 9.6, 10.3, 10.5
Lichen Sclerosis	2.17, 8.2
Lips	2.4, 2.12
Lubrication	2.4, 2.12, 3.3, 4.1, 8.3, 11.1
Mastectomy	3.9
Masturbation	1.5, 2.3, 2.13, 3.2, 3.8, 12.3

Menopause	1.5, 1.10, 2.11, 4.1, 7.11
Menstruation	2.15
Migraine	4.2, 4.3
Nocturnal Penile Tumescence	5.5, 5.12
Obesity	8.4, 8.6
OCD	3.9
Oophorectomy	3.16, 4.1
Oral sex	2.15, 4.5, 5.9, 9.2
Orgasm	1.7, 2.4, 2.5, 2.6, 2.12, 2.17, 3.2, 3.3, 3.6, 3.7, 3.9, 3.10, 3.13, 3.14, 3.16, 3.17, 4.2, 4.5, 5.4, 5.7, 5.8, 5.9, 7.9, 8.1, 8.2, 8.3, 9.3, 9.5, 9.9, 9.11, 10.2, 10.3, 10.6, 10.7, 11.1, 12.3
Panic Disorder	3.9
Parkinson's Disease	8.2, 9.7
Paxil	3.1, 5.4, 8.1
Pelvic Organ Prolapse	4.3, 9.8
Penis	2.4, 3.3, 4.1, 4.3, 5.5, 5.6, 5.8, 5.12, 8.6, 9.7, 11.1

Pessary	9.8
Peyronie's Disease	4.3, 8.6
Pharmaceutical	1.12, 3.1, 8.2, 8.3
Phimosis	4.3
Phosphodiesterase	5.5, 8.2
Plateau phase	3.9, 5.4, 5.8, 8.1, 8.2, 8.3
Premature ejaculation	5.8, 8.2, 10.6
Priapism	4.3, 5.5, 5.6, 8.2, 8.3, 9.7
Progesterone	9.5, 9.13
Prostaglandin	5.5, 8.2
Prostate	1.7, 2.13, 4.3, 5.5, 7.1, 8.7
Prozac	3.2, 5.4, 8.1, 8.3
Psychologist	1.6, 2.14, 7.2, 7.3, 11.1
Psychiatrist	1.6
Pubococcygeus muscles	2.4
PUF questionnaire	4.4
Rape	5.7, 7.2, 8.6, 9.11, 11.1, 12.1
Rectocele	3.3, 4.3, 9.8
Rectum	3.3
Refractory phase	2.4, 2.6, 2.12, 5.8
Resolution phase	2.4

Scrotum	5.5
Sexuality	1.2, 1.4, 1.5, 1.11, 1.14, 2.3, 2.10, 2.11, 2.14, 3.11, 6.1, 7.4, 8.2, 9.2, 9.11,
SSRI	5.8
STI	3.8, 4.3, 5.9, 7.1, 8.5, 10.2, 11.2, 12.1, 12.2
Testosterone	1.7, 2.7, 2.12, 2.16, 2.17, 5.5, 7.3, 7.11, 8.2, 8.6, 9.5, 9.6, 10.4, 10.5, 11.3
Thrust dysporeunia	3.3, 4.1
Urethra	4.4, 5.5
Urination	4.3
Urologist	1.6
Vagina	1.7, 2.3, 2.4, 2.5, 2.12, 2.15, 2.17, 3.1, 3.3, 3.4, 3.5, 3.6, 3.7, 3.8, 3.12, 3.16, 4.1, 4.3, 7.1, 8.2, 9.5, 9.8, 9.12, 10.1, 11.1, 11.2, 12.1

Vaginismus	3.3, 4.3, 9.5
Vaginitis	1.4, 3.3, 10.6
Vestibulitis	3.5
Vibrator	3.2, 4.5, 5.9, 10.2
Vulva	2.12, 3.3, 4.1, 9.5, 9.10, 9.11
Wellbutrin	8.1, 8.2, 8.3
Yeast infection	3.3, 3.4, 4.1, 4.3, 8.2, 10.1
Yohimbine	5.6, 8.2, 8.6
Zoloft	3.1, 5.4, 8.1
Zyban	8.1, 8.2, 8.3

Did you like SeniorSex?

Do you need more copies for friends and relatives? Of course you do! Order directly from the publisher at www.geroproducts.com, through your local bookstore, or use the order form below (may be photocopied). Also, you may be interested in our other books and gifts:

Qty ___  *SeniorSex: Answers to Your Questions from a Geriatric Gynecologist* by Daniel Laury, M.D. - $19.95

This book provides the answers to sexual questions that patients are seeking from their doctors, and is ideal for single seniors and senior couples, as well as doctors and other medical personnel.

Qty ___ *Seniors in Love: A Second Chance for Single, Divorced and Widowed Seniors* by Robert Wolley - $19.95

This well-reviewed book deals with the emotional, financial, physical, and other relevant issues facing seniors when considering a new, intimate relationship.

Qty ___ *The Greatest Companion: Reflections on Life, Love and Marriage After 60* by Robert Wolley - $19.95

Through prose and poetry, this book explores the joys of late-in-life love, provides reminders of what such a love needs to flourish, and reflects upon love's agelessness.

Mom No More: Coping With the Late-Life Loss of Adult Children - One Woman's Story by Mignon Matthews - $29.95

The author lost both of her children after they were adults - her daughter Evie at 18 and her son Albert at 42. This is her story of coping with the depression, pain, anger, and injustice of outliving her beloved children.

Sidewalks in the Jungle: What it's REALLY Like to Retire and Live in Costa Rica by Alfred Stites - $35.95

This book deals with the reality of moving to, and living in htis beautiful and stable Central American democracy. Topics covered span from managing maids and gardeners to trips to the doctor and avoiding violent street crime.

The Healthy Seniors Cookbook: Ideal Meals and Menus for People Over Sixty (Or Any Age) by Marilyn McFarlane - $19.95

Whether cooking for yourself, your spouse, or visiting grandchildren, this book features an easy-to-read, easy-to-use format that provides flavorful meals and simple, fast cooking methods.

ABC's for Seniors: Successful Aging Wisdom from an Outrageous Gerontologist by Ruth Jacobs - $19.95

In this book, Dr. Jacobs presents the essentials that enable a reader to harvest life fully for creative, healthy, successful, vigorous, and meaningful aging.

Qty ___ *Seniors in Love* car magnet - $11.95
Show the world that love knows no age! An ideal wedding or anniversary gift! Measures six by four inches, in red, white, and gold. Removable. Fits any RV!

Qty ___ *"Grow old along with me"* mug - $9.95
Robert Browning said it, but it's as true today as it was 100 years ago! Illustration and quote, printed in black on both sides. Truly, *"the best is yet to be"*

Name _____

Address _____

City/State/Zip _____

Please mark the products you want, and their quantity (Missouri residents only please add 5.25% sales tax).

There is no charge for shipping and handling, and all orders are shipped from Greentop, Missouri (population 427).

Send check or money order to:
Hatala Geroproducts
PO Box 42
Greentop, MO 63546

What makes Hatala Geroproducts different?

Hatala Geroproducts of Greentop, Missouri, was founded in 2002. An independent company, Hatala Geroproducts publishes books, games, magnetic signs, and greeting cards primarily for seniors. The focus is on relationships: with spouses, lovers, other seniors, grandchildren, and adult children.

• All products are "age positive," which means that they are respectful to seniors, and focus on the positive aspects of aging.

• All books are "larger print" for easier reading.

• Books are written by senior authors for senior readers.

• All products are developed with the help of academic gerontologists and seniors themselves.

• Hatala Geroproducts is dedicated to remain an earth-friendly, sustainable, carbon-neutral company.

We thank you for your continued support!

If you have any questions or comments, feel free to contact me personally at mark@geroproducts.com

Mark Hatala, Ph.D.
President, Hatala Geroproducts
Professor of Psychology, Truman State University

CPSIA information can be obtained
at www.ICGtesting.com
Printed in the USA
LVHW01s1444050918
589228LV00004B/581/P